HOW TO LEARN
RUSSIAN
IN 30 DAYS

Chiara Monetti

CONTENTS

Introduction: WELCOME! ДОБРО ПОЖАЛОВАТЬ!

Dear reader, welcome to this course of Russian language! If you are here, it means that you have always wanted to comply with the desire to learn something more about this fascinating eastern language. Let me tell you that you did the right thing!

There are a lot of good reasons why studying Russian nowadays: it is the ninth language in the world for numbers of speakers (according to the survey of the UN in 2007), and besides being a useful tool to travel through Russia, it is also a language with a huge cultural, artistic and literary background. Furthermore its role in the economy is growing more and more. Whatever the reason that brought you here, it is already a good start on which to base your study.

This course is divided into 30 lessons, conceived to be tackled consecutively in one month. I know, you will be thinking that learning Russian in one month is impossible: I can assure you though, that you will be amazed by the number of notions you will learn and the results will be astonishing, thanks to our fast and funny learning method.

You are probably a little scared now that you know what you are going to face. For example, you will be wondering: "How do I read all those weird letters in the title?"

Well, I can promise that in a few days this will be a vague idea.

Step by step together, we will deal with the main aspects of this language, traditionally considered to be really different from ours but very fascinating and interesting. Attention: this course is not just about grammar and phonetics! As a matter of fact, if you really want to be familiar with a language, it is fundamental knowing its cultural roots: for this reason, at the ending of every week, I thought to deal with more relaxing chapters so that you will be able to see the results of your efforts.

Moreover, each time I will add a cultural aspect to a new linguistic content so that you can fix your knowledge to facts, things and people, in order to make the memorization easier. The study of a language is always a challenge, and to win every challenge you need motivation. Whatever motivation, set it in your mind and never lose sight of it: this is the best method to fling yourself in this new adventure with courage.

Now, set aside any kind of uncertainty and be ready to be absorbed by the Russian climate: you won't need snow boots and winter clothes, you will just need a pinch of patience and a strong desire to be amazed.

Are you ready? Let's go!

DAY 1: THE CYRILLIC ALPHABET IS LIKE RIDING A BYCICLE

Do you remember when you learnt how to ride a bycicle? At the beginning the fear of falling was stronger than the desire to try it, then you realized that no one was pushing you anymore and you were going on your own. From that day, you have never forgotten how to do it. Well, the Cyrillic alphabet will be the same for you: from the moment you memorize these letters for the first time, you will never forget them. On the contrary, you will realize that recognizing them is not impossible, you will be able to read them quickly in a rent announcement at the corner of the street or in an advertising at the station. Honestly it won't be easy: all of us fell off the bike, it is important not to lose the desire to pedal!
Now, I am asking you to go back to when you were a child and to "reset" what you know about writing. You will notice that this initial effort will give you a great satisfaction: learning a new alphabet is not a mere trifle!

1.1. Back to school

Russian is an East Slavic language such as Byelorussian and Ukrainian. The languages belonging to this group make use of the Cyrillic alphabet (although there are several variations of it), a writing system dating back to the 9th century AD.

There are two more branches of Slavic languages: the West Slavic ones (Polish, Czech and Slovak) that make use of the whole Latin alphabet with additional letters; and the South Slavic (Serbian, Croatian, Slovene, Montenegrin, Bulgarian and Macedonian) that make use of a mixed Cyrillic and Latin alphabet. Obviously in each group there are also less common languages, but this is not the right time to study a new linguistic notion, so, for now, let's just focus on Russian language and its Cyrillic alphabet.
As years went by, this alphabet developed and it was subjected to modifications until the current form.

Observing with a quick glance the letters of this alphabet, you will notice that it is made of both Latin and Greek letters. Don't worry, it is not necessary to know both languages!

You will probably discover unimaginable letters: is "Ж" a sound or some strange magic sign? And where is the difference between "Ш" and its sister with the little tail "Щ"?

If you really want to learn reading the Cyrillic alphabet, it is important for you to know every single letter to avoid any kind of confusion with our alphabet. For example: "Р" in Russian corresponds to our "R"; "P" is written as "П", like the pi in mathematics.

The Russian Cyrillic alphabet contains 33 letters overall:

- 10 vowels: а, е, ё, и, о, у, ы, э, ю, я
- 21 consonants: б, в, г, д, ж, з, й, к, л, м, н, п, р, с, т, ф, х, ц, ч, ш, щ,
- 2 graphic signs: : ь (soft sign), ъ (hard sign)

Did I muddle your ideas? Don't worry, in the following table you can find a precise explanation of every letter, the pronunciation, the transliteration and an example for each word. Let's see together how to pronounce these words.

Tab. THE CYRILLIC ALPHABET

Cyrillic Letter	Cursive Writing	Pronunciation	Scientific Transliteration	Examples	Translation
А а	*А а*	a	a	аэропорт	airport
Б б	*Б б*	b	b	брат	brother
В в	*В в*	v	v	вагон	wagon
Г г	*Г г*	g (strong)	g	гараж	garage
Д д	*Д д*	d	d	да	yes
Е е	*Е е*	ye as in "yes"	e	есть	to eat
Ё ё	*Ё ё*	yo as in "yolk"	ё	ёж	hedgehog
Ж ж	*Ж ж*	"j" in French word "jour"	zh	жена	wife
З з	*З з*	z as in "zoo"	z	зоопарк	zoo
И и	*И и*	i	i	игра	game
Й й	*Й й*	(short i) as in boy	ĭ	йогурт	yogurt
К к	*К к*	k	k	кошка	cat
Л л	*Л л*	l	l	луна	moon
М м	*М м*	m	m	мама	mom
Н н	*Н н*	n	n	нет	no
О о	*О о*	o (closed)	o	опера	opera
П п	*П п*	p	p	папа	dad
Р р	*Р р*	r	r	Россия	Russia
С с	*С с*	s	s	студент	student
Т т	*Т т*	t	t	туфли	shoes
У у	*У у*	u	u	университет	university
Ф ф	*Ф ф*	f	f	фото	photo
Х х	*Х х*	aspirated cha s in German "Achtung"	kh	характер	character
Ц ц	*Ц ц*	ts as in "tsunami"	ts	цирк	circus
Ч ч	*Ч ч*	ch as in "cheese"	ch	чай	tea
Ш ш	*Ш ш*	sh as in "shock"	sh	шуба	fur
Щ щ	*Щ щ*	shsh as in "fresh sheen" but softer	shch	щётка	hairbrush
ъ	*ъ*	hard sign	-	-	-
ы	*ы*	i (strong)	y	дыр	hole
ь	*ь*	soft sign	-	-	-
Э э	*Э э*	e with the mouth open wider	è	экзамен	exam
Ю ю	*Ю ю*	yu as in "Yukon"	yu	юбка	skirt
Я я	*Я я*	ya as in "Yalta"	ya	яблоко	apple

As you can see, the Russian alphabet contains more letters than our alphabet. Thi is not bad as it may seems: some sounds that in English are pronounced through a group of consonants, in Russian it is possible to write them with a single letter! Isn'it great?

In the following column you can find a sequence of words, each starting with the corresponding letter of the alphabet: let's see how to pronounce them, dividing the alphabet in 4 parts.

I will point out the accent and some general notes for every word, specifying the meaning. Let's go!

аэропорт	aerapórt, "airport" In this case the letter "o" is pronounced as it is written since it is stressed; when it is unstressed, it is pronounced as an "a".
брат	Brat, "brother"
вагон	vagòn, "wagon"
гараж	garàge, pronounced similar to English
да	da, "yes"
есть	iest', "to eat"
ёж	yòzh, "hedgehog" The symbol ж, "zh" is pronounced like the French "j" in the word "jour". From this moment on we will use the letter "j" to point out the symbol ж.
жена	jenà, "wife"
зоопарк	zoopàrk, "zoo" The sound of the symbol "з"corresponds to the sound of the "z" in "zoo".

For now, the Cyrillic alphabet has an order similar to ours but with additional letters that we do not have or we usually see in a different position (v, g, z, j). I am already anticipating some pronunciation rules that we will study in detail in the next lesson, but it is important to be familiar with these words right away so that you can challenge yourself!

Let's study the second part of the alphabet:

игра	igrà, "game"
йогурт	iógurt, "yogurt"
кошка	kóška, "cat" The symbol "š" corresponds to the sound of the "sh" in "shock" but with the tongue farther back in the mouth
луна	lunà, "moon"
мама	màma, "mom"
нет	niét, "no"
опера	ópiera, "opera" Remember that the vowel "o" is always closed!
папа	pàpa, "dad"
Россия	Rassìia, "Russia" The "o" is pronounced "a" when it is unstressed.
студент	studiént, "student"
туфли	tùfli, "shoes"
университет	universitiét, "university"
фото	fóto, "photo"

In this second part of the alphabet there is nothing unusual but the absence of our "q" and the fact that our "v" is replaced by the Russian "f". Be careful though: we are going to enter a jungle filled with new sounds! It seems that the most difficult letters are grouped together here to frighten you: do not let them scare you! Follow the path word by word.

| характер | charàktier, "character" "Ch" is pronounced as an aspirated "c", like in the German word "Achtung". |

цирк	zzirk, "circus" I doubled the "z" to distinguish it from the pronunciation of the letter "з".
чай	ciài, "tea"
шуба	shùba, "fur"
щётка	schyótka, "hairbrush" The sound produced by this letter is more "extended" than the previous one.

The last section of the alphabet consists exclusively of vowels and two phonetic symbols. We will deal with them in the next lessons, now let's focus on the pronunciation of the last four words:

дыр	dir, "hole" The sound is similar to a strong "i" in the English word sin, produced by drawing farther back the tongue; it is a choked sound, a new sound between "u" and "i".
экзамен	ekzàmien, "exam"
юбка	yùbka, "skirt"
яблоко	yàblaka, "apple" The unstressed "o" is pronounced as "a".

At a first reading you probably noticed that it is hard to deeply understand some new sounds, so if you want to practice you should surf the Internet to understand it in a better way. Indeed there are a lot of tools such as useful tutorials on YouTube: they are a good and funny method to learn and practice the language. An alternative method could be recording your voice while you read and then listening again to it at a distance of a few days in order to notice your improvements.

If you are having some difficulties in this first phase, do not lose heart! It is important to point out that, like every other alphabet, letters have specific rules and they link one another by following accurate preferences.

Lastly I want to focus on the column of the table we have not analyzed yet, the column of the scientific transliteration. It is not so particular but it is a useful system for you to reproduce Russian first names by using Latin letters (as well as to verify your knowledge about correct writing: how many versions of the name Gorbachev have you read? And Khrushchev?

Even if the scientific transliteration is correct, it is not helpful for the pronunciation. For this reason in the textbook we will specify clearly how to pronounce the following Russian letters:

ж → j (more properly: zh)
ц → zz (more properly: ts)
х → kh (it is just the same: kh)
ч → ch (it is just the same: ch)

We will study these notions starting from tomorrow. For now I suggest to test what you have learned at this point of the course, writing included: copy the alphabet table and try to read the words of every example.

This is you first day and you have already learned about thirty words: well done!

1.2. Block letters or cursive writing?

You probably noticed that in the table there are two columns of letters, one for block letters and one for cursive writing. There is not a great difference between the two writings, except in some cases. Be careful to the so-called "false friends" shifting from a column to the other.

You just need to know that Russian people make use of the cursive writing when they write by hand, but in every book, on the Internet and above all in this course you will read in block letters.

If you happen to write a letter to your Russian friend, then you can explore that great range of fluttering letters!

Russian handwriting could be difficult to understand at a first glance, but at the same time it is a clear and linear writing, similar to that one that we used to learn at school when we were kids.

To Russians the accuracy and the clarity of the writing is essential. With a good deal of effort you will notice that even your writing will definitely improve: try and see!

Russian Cursive

word "лишишь"

ЛИШИШЬ

лилии, дышишь, дышишь,
лишишься, слышишь,
шишишилли, шишалия.

Russian cursive writing is beautiful, isn't it? Unfortunately there is no time to learn it now because we would need a different kind of study and more time. Although it is interesting the fact that writing is still taught in school and that it is a sort of tradition handed down through generations.

Let's disclose the secrets of th

. The Cyrillic alphabet contai
letters and two phonetic sym¹

. Every single letter has a s
are pretty distant from our

. The alphabet order is similar to ours, exc
tion of a few letters.

. There are different methods to practice, from tutorials on YouTube to the personal practice in reading and writing. Mixing up different methods will help you to test your knowledge in Russian language.

. Understanding where the stress falls is fundamental to pronounce correctly a word: the vowel "o" is pronounced as it is just if it is stressed; if it is unstressed it is pronounced as "a".

. When Russians write by hand they make use of the cursive writing. In other cases you will always find block letters, even if the print font may change.

DAY 2: A SYMPHONY OF NEW SOUNDS

As you noticed studying the alphabet, Russian language has various sounds. Look at yourself in the mirror, warm up with a tongue-twister and let's go! Get ready for your first Russian pronunciation lesson!

Let's find out about what Russians define "Трудные буквы", that is to say "difficult letters" (трудный – trùdny = difficult, буква - bùkva = letter).

2.1. Consonants and double cross

So far we have seen the sounds of the consonants in their common version. Although, you have to know that there are cases in which they change producing a slightly different sound, like a perfect two-faced spy. Take a look at this two words:

Брат (brat) is "brother"
...... but **Брать** (brat') is the verb "to take"

What is the difference between the two? The second one ends with "ь", the "soft sign" (мягкий знак, myagkij znàk), one of the two phonetic symbols of the Russian alphabet. The actual pronunciation of a consonant followed by "ь" is called "soft pronunciation" (or "palatalized"). In our case, as a matter of fact, the consonant is always a "t" but its sound is similar to a "ts" (from now on, to avoid confusion, I will specify it with an apostrophe after the consonant, **t'**). You will often find the soft sign in Russian words. On the contrary, its older brother "ъ", hard sign (твёрдый знак, tvyórdyj znàk) is more rare, it "strengthens" the sound of the consonant it accompanies, avoiding a softer sound and creating a little pause between the two sounds in which it is inserted.

Try to read these words with the two phonetic symbols:

мать = (mat') mother
ночь = (noc') night
ель = (iel', soft sound) spruce

объём = (ab"yóm) volume
субъект = (sub"iékt) subject
инъекция = (in"iékziya) injection

I will tell you a secret: palatalization (or rather the pronunciation of a sound with the tongue drawn up farther toward
the palate), is a common phenomenon in a lot of languages,
even in English. In English the "ny" in the word "canyon"
could approximately produce the effect of a palatalized
sound. You will probably find similarities with the Russian
letters "н"end "л" and the addition of the soft sign:

try to guess, what does "ньокки" mean? (Answers at the end
of the chapter)

The soft sign is just one of the two methods to make a consonant sound softer. In order to understand when to pronounce a "soft" sound you have to look at the following
vowel. For example:

да (da) = yes   дядя (d'iàd'ya) = uncle

In the first case the "d" is pronounced as a normal "d". On
the contrary, in the second word the "d" is pronounced as a
consonant accompanied by the soft sign. As we will immediately study, vowels have an essential role in Russian.
But let's recap quickly:

consonant + soft sign ь = soft pronunciation
consonant + soft vowel (я, е, и, ё, ю) = soft pronunciation

In the other cases the consonant pronunciation is hard. Ini-
tially the hard sign was used as opposed to the soft sign,
more properly at the end of the word, where a hard sign was
being inserted.
Nowadays this use disappeared for a more linguistic practi-
cality, especially thanks to the recent linguistic reform en-
couraged by the Revolution in 1918. Russian students are

grateful to the Bolsheviks, since they have really simplified the Russian orthography!

2.2. Hard and soft vowels

So, I have already anticipated the existence of the "soft" vowels. Differently from consonants, they do not "switch mood" so easily: a leopard can't change its spots, and that is the same for the hard and soft nature of vowels. Let's take a look at the two and some advice to pronounce them (pronounciation is in brackets):

hard vowels: а (a) − э (è) − ы (hard i) − о (closed o) − у (u)
soft vowels: я (yà) − е (ié, closed) − и (i) − ё (yó, always stressed) − ю (iù)

This general scheme can help you memorize the ten vocalic sounds, even if we need to point out some rules:

1) The letter э is only present at the beginning of the word (or in loan words from other languages); so the Russian sound "e" is largely pronounced as "ye", with a closed "e". That is the reason why Russians cannot easily pronounce the open "e"!

Try to read: **аэропорт** (aeraport, airport), **экономика** (ekanomika, economy), **это** (eta, this).

2) What is ы? How can an "i" be hard? Maybe it is the strangest sound when it comes to pronounce it, but with a little practice we can easily reproduce it.

Some words to practice: **дыр** (dyr, hole), **быть** (byt', to be), **мыть** (myt', to wash)

The sound of this vowel is produced starting from the throat and it produces this chocked sound between "u" and "i". To find the right spot, start pronunciating a long "u" and then

with your lips in that position start pronunciating the "ï".
Don't worry if you cannot reproduce this sound: Russians
understand our phonetic difficulties and they will try to help
you anyway! Just be careful to distinguish it from the sound
of a normal "i" (the letter **И**): a difference of sound that
changes the meaning, from "to be" (**быть**) to "to beat"
(**бить**)!

3) Both "o" and its soft sister "ё" correspond with a closed
"o". Important: when you speak Russian, forget the existence of the open "ò", it is an unknown sound to them! You
can practice speaking like a "proper Russian": transform all
your "o"s in super closed "uo"s. Try fuor a whuole day.
(And say thank you to your friends for their patience!).

4) As you have already seen with the pronunciation of the
words of the alphabet, the "ё" is always stressed; when the
"o" is unstressed it is pronounced as an "a": the word
шофёр (driver, from French chauffeur) can help you remember both grammar rules because it is pronounced
"sciafiór".

2.3. Dislikes between vowels and consonants: the groups of Г, К, Х and Ж, Ш, Ч, Щ

Now let's analyze some specific consonant groups that sound really strange for our pronunciation standards.

1) First group is Г, К and Х. It is a normal group of consonants that produce hard sounds: let's take a look again at the words from chapter 1 (have you tried memorizing them?)

Гараж (garàj)
Кошка (kóshka)
Характер (kharàkter)

If we are familiar with the first two sounds, we have to focus on the sound produced by "Х": try to make the final part of the palate vibrate, like if you are gargling. That is the right method to pronounce "Х".
You also need to know one last thing about this first group: they have dislikes towards some vowels, with which they never link. In Russian you won't find these combinations:

Г, К, Х never link to Я, Э, Ы, Ё, Ю
(because it is impossible to pronounce them)

Such combination is possible just in foreign words transliterated in Cyrillic (a common phenomenon)…

how will you dress this year at Хэллоуин?

…or in first names and place names with a foreign origin: Гюнтер (Günther), Кёльн (Köln, Colonia)

2) Let's see the second group, Ж, Ш, Ч, Щ. They are called "palatal" consonants and they are divided into two catego-

ries: hard and soft. Be careful though, unexpectedly the "soft" ones will give you a hard time.

Let's see again the examples we have already studied:

Жена (jenà); Шуба (shùba); Чай (ciài); Щётка (shchótka)

Two of them, Ж e Ш, produce hard sounds, harder than those you already know (the French "j" for example). To become a perfect Russian try to pronounce these sounds with the front part of the mouth, rounding forward the lips.
Try to pronounce these words: **журнал** (jurnàl, magazine), **муж** (muj, husband), **шар** (shar, ball), **шкаф** (shkaf, cabinet).

The other two letters, Ч e Щ, are similar to "ch" in the word "cheese" or "sh" in "fresh", but softer. To practice extend these sounds rising high the tongue towards the palate, just as we have studied for the soft consonants.
Test yourself: **часть** (ciàst', part), **чудо** (ciùda, miracle), **тёща** (tiòshcha, mother-in-law), **щи** (lo shchi, a traditional Russian soup made with cabbage).

It is important to point out the difference between Ш and Щ: try to distinguish the two sounds "strengthening" the first one.

2.4. That bizarre Ц

The letter Ц is also a particular sound jus as Ж and Ш; it is a strong"z", similar to the "ts" in English "nuts". Differently from its friends, Ц "acts tough even with tough guys": it can go with the hard "i" ("ы") and also with the normal "и", but the final result in pronunciation will always be the hard "ы".

If you happen to go to the circus in Russia, get ready to pronounce цирк as a chocked sound. Don't worry if it seems you have hiccups: they will understand you!

2.5. Consonant reduction, or phonetic 3x2

For now, we have seen the main sounds of Russian language taken singularly. You will happen to bump into apparently unpronounceable words containing random consonants: for example, a word like **приветствовать** could scare you at first (when it simply means "to greet"!). So, how do we unravel that consonant mess?

By taking advantage of the consonant reduction! Russians do not have superpowers to pronounce such words!

Here the main consonant nexus and their precise pronunciation:

. the groups сч/ зч/ жч are pronounced as a щ (sch, soft sound):

Ex. счастье   (schàst'ie, happiness), мужчина (muschìna, man)

. the groups дц/ тц/ тс / тьс are pronounced as ц (ts):

Ex. отца (atsà, father, genitive case), смеяться (smieiàtsa, to laugh)

You need practice when it comes to reproduce Russian sounds, so we will keep doing it in the other lessons. As in every new language that you start studying from zero, the fundamental elements are the effort and the desire to put yourself in the game!

Let's disclose the secrets of this chapter

. Russian consonants and vowels can be divided in two large groups: hard and soft.

Tab. 2: CONSONANTS AND VOWELS

hard	б в г д з л м н п р с т ф х (followed by a hard vowel or, rarely, hard sign) + а э ы о у + ъ	ж ш ц	
soft	б в г д з л м н п р с т ф х (followed by a soft vowel and/or soft sign) + я е и ё ю + ь		ч щ

. In order to pronounce soft consonants you have to raise the tongue toward the palate.

. <

. Even if vowels are more numerous thn ours, they are well definedand they link to some types of consonants in particular ways (the "hard ones" ж ш ц and the "soft ones" ч щ).

. Be careful when it comes to point out the different sound between the two consonants ш and щ (also written likewise): think about the English "sh" in "shock" and strengthen it to pronounce ш, and pronounce it softer to make щ.

. The best trick to practice your pronunciation is doing it while you are in front of a mirror.

ANSWERS.

<u>Ньокки</u> means "gnocchi" (small Italian dumplings);

<u>Хэллоуин</u> is Halloween!

The aspirated "h" that you can find in other languages (English, German, Chinese, etc.) in Russian is expressed through the letters x or г. Other examples are:

Гарри Поттер = Harry Potter
холдинг = holding
Хенри = Henry

DAY 3: MEET THE ENEMY

Today we are going to focus on something more practical, so that you can test what you have learned until now. Let's study how to face a first brief conversation in Russian, obviously starting from the basic passages: greeting, introducing yourself, saying thank you.

Did you know about the Russian version of Winnie The Pooh? Its name is Винни Пух (Vinni Pukh) and in this cartoon it seems a little doubtful about the entity of its interlocutor:

"Piataciòk (Russian Piglet), this looks like a weird exemplar of bear...".
You do not want to create a negative impression when you introduce yourself to a Russian, don't you?

3.1. How to greet

Unlike English, in Russian there are two ways to address people, based on the different level of formality:
- you can use the familiar "you" (ты, "ty") when you talk to friends and family members;
-

you can use the formal "you" (in Russian вы "vy") when addressing two or more people or a person in authority or higher in years or status.

It is important to understand the difference between the two. In Russian it is customary for adults using the formal form "вы" when they first meet
Let's see some type of greeting to start a conversation:

Привет!

"Привет!" (privièt)= hello , for friends and people you know well.

Здравствуйте!

"Здравствуйте" (sdràsvuitie)= hi, more formal than Привет.

"Привет!"(priviét) = hello, referred to friends and people we know.
"Здравствуйте" (sdràsvuitie) = hi, a little more formal than привет.

Does this last word look like a tangle of impossible consonants? Don't worry, you will often hear something like "sdràstie!"(здрасьте!), a more colloquial form (and easier!): you can use it in a less official context, but the meaning is the same.
So, it is important to understand how to handle the situation right away: "на ты или на вы?"(na ty ili na vy?, familiar o formal you?). It depends on the degree of formality ypu want to use with your Russian interlocutor.

Both привет/здравствуйте are correct in every situation when it comes to meet someone. Obviously, as it happens in other languages, in Russian you can find different greetings for every moment of the day.
Let's see some types of situation in which you can find yourself:

1. You leave home early in the morning to go to work. The first person you meet is the janitor of your building. Since he is just an acquaintance of yours, you can decide to say hi to him using **"Здравствуйте!"** adding his name: "Здравствуйте Антон!"(Sdràsvuitie, Antón).
Since it is early in the morning, you can also use a cordial **"Доброе утро!"**(dóbraie ùtra), that means "Good morning!".

2. Carrying on with your day, once arrived at work, you meet your colleagues or some new client. The Russian morning is until 9 o'clock, so approximately from that time on you can use a different greeting. Clearly, with your trusty colleagues

you can use the good old "**Привет**" (priviét, hi), but if you want to be more formal, it is better making use a more neuter "**Добрый день!**"(dóbry dien'), meaning "good morning!". This type of greeting is really useful: you can use it for the rest of the day until the evening! During the evening in Russian you can use the same greetings of the day.

3. So it is time to leave work and to come back home. At this point we have to distinguish formal and informal greetings. When you say hi to your friend and colleague Ivan, as in every informal situation, you can use "**Пока!**"(pakà), that means again "hello" like привет, but in the moment you leave. On the contrary, if you greet your boss or a person with which you have a formal relationship, it is better using a common expression: the famous "**до свидания**" (da svidània), that means "goodbye". Literally it means "to a next rendezvous", "see you next time". In a not working context, you can also use "**до скорого**" (da skórava, with a pronunciation that does not correspond to the spelling, and we will study why), that means "see you". Leaving work, you can use "**до завтра**" (da zàvtra), "see you tomorrow", since you know you will see your colleagues the next day.

4. Once you left work, you remember you have to buy something to eat for dinner. It is evening, but don't worry: in the largest cities supermarkets are open 24 hours a day! In a shop you can use "**Добрый вечер!**"(dóbry viécher), "good evening", and when you leave the grocery shop you can use again "**до свидания**".

5. Here one last situation: "goodnight" in Russian is used just before going to bed, and it is a little more complicated than the other greetings. "**Спокойной ночи**" (spakòinai nochi), literally means "a quiet night" and it is a less used ex-

pression in comparison with others, since it is used in private situations.

EXERCISE 1

So, let's recapitulate: could you distinguish in what moment of the day these conversations take place? (The answers at the end of the chapter)

1. "Здравствуйте Антон!" (Sdràsvuitie, Antòn)
- Доброе утро, Михайл Иванович!(Dòbrae ùtra, Mikhail Ivànavich)
(We are going to study how Russian first names work in a few lessons!)

2. - Добрый день, Иван! (Dòbryi dién', Ivàn)
- Добый день, Павел.(Dòbryi dién', Pàviel)

3. - До свидания, коллеги! (Da svidània, kalliéghi)
- До завтра, Михайл Иванович!(Da sàvtra, Mikhail Ivànavich)

4. - Добый вечер.(Dòbryi viécher)
- - Добый вечер.(Dòbryi viécher)

5. - Спокойной ночи, Миша. (Spakóinainóchi, Misha)
- - Спокойной ночи, милая. (milaia, = my dear) (Spakóinainóchi, mìlaia)

3.2. Let's introduce ourselves!

Greetings are the key to establish a first contact with Russians. Once exceeded this first step, we can study some useful sentences to introduce yourself!
Let's start from the basis: how to say your name. In English we say "my name is…"; the Russian equivalent is slightly different but it has the same meaning:

"**Меня зовут...**" (minyà zavùt = "they call me")

So, when you introduce yourself in Russian, the whole sentence could be:

"**Привет!**" "**Меня зовут Кьяра!** (Priviet! Minyà zavùt Kiara!)

Obviously the initial greeting can change depending on the situation, as we have already seen, but the sentence "меня зовут" is always the same.
Once you have introduced yourself, you would like to know your interlocutor's name I guess, so, you will ask him/her:

"**Как тебя зовут?**"(Kak tibyà zavùt?), literally "How do they call you?""
"**Как вас зовут?**"(Kak vas zavùt?), "What is your name?"(using the formal you)

Another information you could share at a first meeting is your origin:
"**Меня зовут Кьяра! Я из Англии.** (Yà is Anglii = I am from England)

You can say this sentence using different expressions:
"**Я –англичанка**" (yà anglichanka)= I am English (female)
"**Я –англичанин**" (yà anglichanin)= I am English (male)

43

v your interlocutor's native land you can

da ty? = Where are you from?)
‗‗‗‗da vy? = Where are you from?, using
normal you)

Here some answers you might hear from a Russian: can you
guess the meaning? (The answers at the end of the chapter)

Я – русский / русская (yà rùsskii / rùsskaya)
Я из России (Yà is Rassii)
Я из Москвы / Санкт-Петербурга (Yà is Maskvì / Sankt-
Pieterbùrga)

If you want to point out from which city you come from,
there is a specific grammar rule that you have to study
(Санкт-Петербург changes in Санкт-Петербурга because it
is declined in genitive case). It is not a big deal since a lot of
city names cannot be translated in Russian and they do not
undergo grammar changes (they remain neutral words).

For convenience, I made a list of different city names:

Рим (Rim = Rome) → Я из Рима
Милан (Milàn = Milano) → Я из Милана
Минск (Minsk= Minsk) → Я из Минска
Киев (Kiev= Kiev) → Я из Киева
Лондон (London= London) → Я из Лондона
Нью-Йорк (N'yu-Jork= New York) → Я из Нью-Йорка
Париж (Parizh= Paris) → Я из Парижа

44

If you come from another city, don't worry: its name is simply transliterated in Russian (ex. Abu Dhabi becomes Абу-Даби and the last letter does not change since to Russians, it is a foreign name as we have already seen).

So, you can follow this scheme to introduce yourself in Russian:

Меня зовут (your name).– Minià savùt (your name)
Я –англичанин/ англичанка.– Yà anglichanin / anglichanka
Я из (your city declined in genitive case).Ya is (your city declined in genitive case).
"Как тебя зовут?" "Откуда ты?"– Kak tibià savùt? Atkùda ty?

(you can also use the formal "you": "Как вас зовут?" Откуда вы?, Kak vas savùt?, Atkùda vy?)

Lastly, here a useful sentence to impress the person you are talking to: after introducing yourself, you can say "**Очень приятно!**"(Ochin' priàtna), "nice to meet you". If you use this sentence you will definitely cut a fine figure!

EXERCISE 2

Take a look at this brief dialogue between these two characters, Ivan and Irina:

SENTENCE	PRONUNCIATION	TRANSLATION
Здравствуй, Иван!	Sdràsvui, Ivàn!	Hi, Ivan!
Привет, Ирина!	Privièt, Irina!	Hello Irina!
Как дела?	Kak dielà?	How are you?
Спасибо, хорошо.	Spasiba, kha-rashò.	Good, thank you.
А у тебя?	A u tibià?	And you?
Нормально.	Narmàlna.	Normal.

Now, try to complete the two following brief dialogues: the answers at the end of the chapter.

1. Evening meeting:

-...................................... Сергей Михайлович!	-,...................................... Sierghièi Mikhàilovich!
- Добрый................................, Мария Ивановна!	-Dòbry................................Marìa Ivanovna!
-Как.........?	-Kak.........?
-Всё в порядке. А...............?	-Vsiò v paryàdke. A.........?
-Хорошо, спасибо.	-Kharashò, spasiba.

2. Introducing yourself:

-Здравствуй! Меня............. Коля.	-Sdràsvui! Minyà.................Kolya.
-Привет! Я Марко..............ты?	-Privièt! Ya Marko.........ty!
-Я из Москвы. А ты?	-Yà is Maskvy. A ty?
-А я....... Лондона.	-A yà....... Londona.
-В Англии! Как интересно! Я в...........еще не бывал. А ты бывал в ....?	-V Anglii! Kak intierièsna! Yà v...... ishò niè byval. A ty byval v.........?
-В России никогда не бывал.	-V Rossii nikagdà nie byvàl.

Notes about the meaning:

1. **Всё в порядке** = an
ok", literally "everything

2. **Как интересно!**
ferent meanings. This is
еще не бывал = I have neve
никогда не бывал = I have never b

You will find the complete translation and the answ
end of the chapter.

3.3. Thank yo

As in ever
those fur
you, yo
Mayb
use

language, in Russian it is important to know all
damental words for every situation: yes, no, thank
u're welcome, excuse me.
e you have already heard some of them since they are
d almost everyday. Let's study them together!

Let's start with the simple "yes" and "no", that you have already seen in the initial table:
ДА (da) means "yes"
НЕТ (niet) means "no"

You won't need roundabout expressions for these concepts: Russians are direct and determined people when it comes to choices. Try not to reply twice "yes, yes" or "no, no". This repetition is an exaggeration to them.

The apparent tough temper of Russian people does not mean that they do not appreciate courtesy: when they understand that you are putting all your effort to speak Russian to establish a contact with them, then they begin demonstrating their appreciation!
A great word that you must never forget to say in every situation is "thank you" (even in English it is important!).
The basic word to thank someone in Russian is **СПАСИБО** (spasìba, thank you), to which you can add other words depending on your degree of gratitude, for example:

большое спасибо, or спасибо большое (bal'sciòie spasìba – thank you so much)
огромное спасибо (agrómnaie spasìba – thanks a lot)

сердечное спасибо (sierdiéchnaie spasìba – heartfelt thanks, just in the written form)

Once you have thanked someone, you have two options: you can simply nod and it means "you're welcome" not expressed in words; or you can say **не за что** (niézaschto), meaning the same "you're welcome". This is a typical Russian expression composed of short words pronunciated as they were a single word. We are going to study other examples in chapter 29.

Another word to say "you're welcome" is **ПОЖАЛУЙСТА** (pajàlusta). This is a useful word because it has another similar meaning, that is to say "please": for example, if you want to give a courtesy tone to a question you can add "pajàlusta" at the beginning or at the end of it.

Как вас зовут, пожалуйста? (Kak vas savùt, pajàlusta?)
Пожалуйста, откуда ты? (Pajàlusta, atkùda ty?)

A typical expression used before questions or requests is **Скажите, пожалуйста…** (Skajìtie, pajàlusta…), meaning "Tell me, please".

Lastly, in addition to "thank you" and "you're welcome", you also need to know how to apologize: there are different ways to do that…

ПРОСТИТЕ (prastìtie) = "excuse me", when you ask for something
ИЗВИНИТЕ (isvinìtie) = "excuse me", similar to "prastìtie"

ПОЖАЛУЙСТА (again!) = "please", always as a courtesy request
МНЕ ЖАЛКО (mnie jàlka) = "I am sorry"

The position of "pajàlusta" inside the sentence is rather free, on the contrary "prastìtie" and "isvinìtie" must be placed always at the beginning:

ex.   Простите / Извините, который час?= excuse me, what time is it?

Differently from other expressions, мне жалко is used to express a true displeasure when a person you are talking to is in a bad situation:

ex.   Ты плохо? Мне жалко! (Ty plokha? Mnie jàlka!) =Are you sick? I am so sorry!

3.4. Smile, yes or no?

Dear reader, at this point, it is important to know something more about Russians' temper. There is a fundamental aspect in their culture that non-Russian people scarcely understand. Since you decided to study Russian language, you should definitely know that Russians do not smile easily. Yes, that is right, you got it right!

Yet, beneath this behavior considered to be "cold", there is a hidden cultural tradition with a specific and interesting meaning.

First of all, **smiling is not considered a courtesy gesture**. Since they consider smiling a spontaneous and genuine gesture towards family members and friends, using it in a different situation becomes a sign of falsehood.

Someone who works does not smile because he/she has absolutely no reason to do that. This kind of behavior does not change when a foreign speaker is around.

So, the Russian smile is a rare phenomenon.

Do not let this fact discourage you! It really is a cultural trait that could wrong-foot you, but you have to understand and accept it.

So, what do we do with our smile? To us smiling is a courtesy gesture and it stands for kindness, and I know that it is difficult to get rid of it as well as it wouldn't be fair to abandon our tradition. The right thing to do could be "reduce" our smile, for example not showing our teeth (Russians call it in a derogatory manner лошадная улыбка,"lashàdnaya ulìbka", horse smile).

It is important to stress the fact that Russians getting closer and closer to the contemporary and international scene and they are starting to integrate foreign customs in their culture. As a matter of fact, smiling seems to be popular again above all with shop assistants in western stores chains.

Maybe, though, it is better knowing that you conquered a spontaneous Russian smile rather than seeing a fake one for the circumstances reassuring you: that is when you know you won their heart.

3.5. How are you? Normal.

Considering what we have learned about "smiling", you won't be surprised knowing that the common answer to the question "How are you?" is "Normal".
This is another concept belonging to the typical Russian temper: **why do I have to answer "I am good" if basically I feel the same like every other day?**
To us it could be an extremely intricate reasoning, but you cannot deny that it is a logical thinking.
The question to ask "how are you?" can be expressed in two ways:
Как дела? (kak dielà?) = literally, how is your business?
or
Как ты? / Как вы? (kak ty? kak vy?) how are you? / how are you? (formal you)

The answers can change according to this scheme:

+++ **очень хорошо / отлично** (ocen' kharasciò / atlichna) = very well, perfect
++ **хорошо** (kharasciò) = good
+ **НОРМАЛНО** (narmàlna) = NORMAL
- **плохо** (plòkha) = badly
- - - **совсем плохо / ужасно**(savsiémplòkha / ujàsna) = terribly, awfully

We can say that more or less the Russian "narmàlna" corresponds to our "good", not entirely sincere to the question "how are you?".

Russians are specialized in creating new expressions about the "how are you?" question, so you could get different answers. Just do not be surprised by their fatalist way to conceive the world: it is a part of their nature!

53

EXERCISE 3

Here I recommend two dialogues, a little more complicated and also closer to the actual speech. I have underlined the new words and the most characteristic expressions. Try translating them, taking a look at the right pronunciation. As always, the answers are at the end of the chapter.

1.
- <u>Приветик</u>, Танечка!
- - Добрый день, Иван!
- А это мой брат Виктор. <u>Рад вас познакомить</u>. Витя, это Таня, моя подруга.
- Очень приятно, Виктор.
- <u>И меня</u> очень приятно, Танечка.

- Priviétik Tàniechka!
- Dòbryi diégn Ruslàn
- A èta moi brat Viktar. Rad vas pasnakòmit'. Vìtia eta Tània, maià padrùga.
- Ociegn priàtna, Vìktar.
- I minià òciegn priàtna, Tàniechka.

2.
- Здравствуйте! <u>Давайте познакомимся</u>. Меня зовут СергейПетрович.
-А Как вас зовут? - <u>Расскажите немного о себе</u>.
- Я американец, из Вашингтона, мне 20 лет, изучаю русский язык в университете в Волгограде.
- <u>К вам лучше обращаться</u> на "вы" или "ты"?
- На "ты".
- <u>Рад с тобой познакомиться</u>.
- Я <u>тоже</u>.

- Sdràsvuitie! Davàitie pasnakòmimsia. Minià savùt Sierghiéi Pitròvich. A kak vas savùt?
- Minià savùt Ben.
- Rasskajìtie nimnòga a sibié.
- Yà amerikàniez, is Vashingtòna, mnié 20 liét, isuchàiu rùsskij iazìk v universitiétie v Volgogràdie.
- K vam lùcce abrashàzza na ty ili na vy?
- Na ty.
- Rad s tabòi pasnakòmizza.
- Yà tòje.

Let's disclose the secrets of this chapter

. When you speak to someone you have to decide whether using informal or formal "you", ты and вы (ty and vy).

. You have to use different kind of greetings depending on the moments of the day. Remember that they also depend on the degree of formality between you and your interlocutor.

. You can introduce yourself by saying your first name and your country: "Привет!" Меня зовут (first name), я англичанин / англичанка. Я из (your city declined in genitive case).

. Saying thank you is important! The two magic words for kindness are **спасибо** (spasiba) "thank you" and **пожалуйста** (pajàlusta), "you're welcome".

. In Russia smiling is not the passe-partout of courtesy, on the contrary sometimes it is considered inappropriate. Do not think that the cashier is mad at you: he/she is just doing his/her job!

. To the question "how are you?" Russians vaguely answer "narmàlna": their "normal" corresponds to our generic "good".

ANSWERS.

Exercise 1
1. Early in the morning: "Hello Anton!" - "Good morning Michajl Ivanovich!"
2. During the day: "Good morning Ivan!" - "Good morning Pavel".
3. Leaving work: "Goodbye colleagues!" - "See you tomorrow, Michajl Ivanovich"
4. An evening meeting: "Good evening"- "Good evening"
5. Before going to bed: "Good night Misha" – "Good night my dear"

Я – русский / русская > I am Russian (male / female)
Я из России > I am from Russia‚
Я из Москв**ы** / Санкт-Петербург**а**> I am from Moscow / Saint Petersburg

Exercise 2
1. Добрый вечер / Здравствуйте; вечер; дела; вы.
translation:
- Good evening, Serghei Mikhailovic!
- Good evening, Maria Ivanovna.
- How are you? (formal you)
- Everything is ok. And you? (again formal you)
- Good, thanks.

2. зовут; Откуда; из; Италии; России.
translation:
- Good morning! My name is Kolya (diminutive of Nikolaj).
- Hi! I am Marco. Where are you from?
- I come from Moscow. And you? (informal you)
- I come from Florence.

- In Italy! Wonderful! I have never been in Italy yet. And have you ever been in Russia?
- No, I have never been in Russia.

Exercise 3

1. particular expressions

Приветик = diminutive of "hello". How can we say it in English? There is not a precise translation. Russians love diminutives, even if the result is a nonsense word.

Рад вас познакомить = pleased to meet you

И меня = me too (speech)

translation:
- Hi Tania! (Taniechka is the hypocorism of Tania, deriving from Tat'iana. We are going to study Russian first names in a few chapters!)
- Good morning Ruslan!
- And this is my brother Viktor. Pleased to meet you. Vitia (diminutive of Viktor), this is my friend Tania.
- Nice to meet you, Viktor.
- Nice to meet you too, Tania.

2. particular expressions

Давайте познакомимся = let's introduce ourselves

Расскажите немного о себе = tell me something about you

К вам лучше обращаться = how I address you

Рад с тобой познакомиться = happy to meet you

тоже = also

translation:
- Good morning! (Let's introduce ourselves) My name is Serghei Petrovich. What is your name? (formal you)
- My name is Ben.

- Tell me something about you.
- I am American, from Washington, I am 20 years old and I study Russian at the Volgograd University.
- How do I address you, with the informal or the formal "you"?
- With the formal "you"
- Pleased to meet you!
- Me too

DAY 4: A WORLD DIVIDED IN THREE: MASCULINE, FEMININE OR NEUTER?

4.1. Three families of words

Dear reader, I want to start this lesson by giving you a great news: Russian has no articles! So, forget about the differences between definite and indefinite article and forget to introduce the words by using them.

Now, I have to dampen your enthusiasm and say that Russian nouns are divided into three large families: **MASCULINE, FEMININE AND NEUTER**

Every word belongs to one of these large categories and, in order to classify them, you must observe the final letter in the basic form of the word, that is to say in the nominative case (we will focus on this soon):

1) <u>MASCULINE:</u> брат, вагон and гараж are all masculine names. What do they have in common? They all end with a consonant. As a matter of fact, this is the first rule to distinguish the nouns of this first group: if the last letter is a consonant, then the word is a masculine noun.
Other examples of masculine nouns taken from our initial table are:
ёж, зоопарк, йогурт, студент, университет, характер, чай, цирк, дыр, экзамен.

2) <u>FEMININE:</u> жена, игра е кошка are feminine nouns. Similarly you have to focus on the last letter: if it is a A or a Я (ya), then the word is a feminine noun. Here the other feminine nouns from the initial list: луна, мама, опера, Россия, шуба, щётка, юбка.

3) <u>NEUTER:</u> this a new gender that most languages do not have. яблоко and море (mòrie, sea) are neuter nouns. The rule to identify these words is always the same, focus on the last letter: if it ends with the vowels "e" or "o", then it is a neuter noun. письмо (pismò, letter), бюро (biurò, office), здание (sdànie, building) are neuter nouns.

<u>Attention!</u> The fact that a noun is neuter does not mean that it must necessarily be inanimated, since inanimated nouns can be masculine and feminine too. For example, in Russian the words "program" (программа) and "love" (любовь) are feminine, the word "pencil" (карандаш) is masculine, the word "window" (окно) is neuter. This is all about the ending of a word and never about the meaning (except for a few cases in which the logical meaning can help you determine the gender, but we will study it in a bit).

You can use this three basic rules to identify which gender a noun belongs to, restricting the field to the singular form: when nouns are plural (or declined in a specific case) they end differently. We will analyze it better in lesson 6 when we will focus on cases.

Let's recap how to determine the gender of a noun:

Final consonant = MASCULINE
A / Я in the ending = FEMININE
O / E in the ending = NEUTER

There is another last case we need to focus on: the soft sign "ь". To determine the gender of the words ending with this sign you cannot follow the previous scheme: you have to observe with which consonant this sign is combined. This is the general rule:

-дь / -ть / -чь = feminine
ex. тетрадь (tietràd', notebook), мать (mat', mother), дочь (doc', daughter)

-нь / -ль = masculine
ex. день (dién', day), читатель (chitàtiel', reader)

Furthermore, the words ending with Ж, Ш, Щ or Ч followed by the soft sign are always feminine; on the contrary, without the soft sign are masculine. We have already studied these consonants (Ж, Ш, Щ and Ч) two chapters ago, and they correspond to the most difficult sounds of this language.

By now everything seems to be clear, but, what language has no exceptions? Already with the soft sign at the end of the word we enter a territory full of quicksands where everything can change in a second. The more you become familiar with the words of a language though, the more you can distinguish them in one of the three categories.

4.2. The exception proves the rule

Exceptions are the language students' daily bread. At first they could seem a real drag, but they actually are useful pretexts to remind you even better the rule that they confirm. We have discussed how a soft sign at the end of a noun can be tricky. Now, let's see other logical exceptions:

папа (pàpa, dad) ends with A, so it should be feminine

This is illogical if we focus on the meaning of the noun, and for this reason it is considered as a masculine noun (this is the same case of дядя, diàdia, "uncle", and дедушка, diédushka, "granpa").
After all the language matches in a flexible way to practical situations.

There are also more enigmatic words when it comes to determine their gender: for example, those nouns ending with the soft sign, as we have already mentioned at the end of the last chapter. In the generic scheme I gave you, there are these exceptions:

дождь (dojd') = rain → MASCULINE
шинель (shiniél') = overcoat (also the title of the famous short story by Gogol) → FEMININE

I f you find a soft sign and you are having doubts about the gender, you can look it up in a dictionary.

In order to learn definitively the gender of these difficult nouns I have found a useful method; try to study them by matching them with adjectives:
ex. сильный дождь, sìlnyi dòjd', heavy rain
тёплая шинель, tiòplaya sciniél', warm overcoat

We are going to analyze adjectives in a few chapters.

4.3. Words without any gender

To make you breath a sigh of relief again as at the beginning of the chapter, I tell you that there also nouns "without any gender" that cannot be a part of the three categories. These nouns are the foreign words imported in the language, transliterated by using Cyrillic letters. Once transliterated they undergo the process that we have just learned: we have to observe the last letter and then decide which gender they belong to.

So, for example, митинг mìting (meeting) becomes masculine, and кафе (kafé, "cafè") becomes neuter.
What do we do with the noun шоу (shòu, "show")?

Other examples are: такси, метро, пальто, бюро – respectively "taxi, subway, coat, bureau (office)".
Well, with these exceptions that do not follow any rule, we have to consider the nouns as neuter or if anything, masculine.

This argument will come in extremely handy in a few lessons.

EXERCISE 4

Try identifying the gender of these nouns: the answers at the end of the chapter.

1. роза (ròsa)= rose	2. стол (stol)= table
3. бар (bar)= bar	4. дискотека (diskatièka)= discotheque
5. задание (sadànie)= exercise	6. Китай (Kitài)= China
7. перо (pierò)= feather	8. клиника (klìnika)= clinic
9. семья (sem'ià)= family	10. катание (katànie)= skating
11. мальчик (màl'chik)= boy	12. доброта (dabratà)= kindness
13. сыр (syr)= cheese	14. папа (pàpa)= dad
15. тетя (tiòtia)=aunt	16. сын (syn)= son

Let's disclose the secrets of this chapter

. In Russian there are three genders: masculine, feminine and neuter.

. You have to focus on the last letter in order to understand which gender a noun belongs to: if it is a consonant then the noun is masculine, if it is a A / Я then it is feminine, if it is O / E then it is neuter.

. The soft sign complicates the situation: it is better memorizing the gender of a word ending with this sign. There is a general scheme, but there are also a lot of exceptions.

. There are words that could seem feminine but according to the logic they are masculine.

. All the exceptions that do not follow the rule are probably nouns imported from other languages. They are considered as neuter nouns and they are also uninflected (indeclinable)

. All these rules are needed to determine the gender of the noun just in nominative case. If a noun is declined in a case, it must be brought back to his singular nominative so that you can understand its gender.

ANSWERS.

Exercise 4

1. F
2. M
3. M
4. F
5. N
6. M
7. N
8. F
9. F
10. N
11. M
12. F
13. M
14. M
15. F
16. M

DAY 5: IN RUSSIAN THERE IS NO "TO BE" AND "TO HAVE"

Dear reader, today I want to give you another great news that will definitively simplify your journey inside the Russian language. But before explaining what this is about, I want to show you a sentence that you have already learned:

"Я –англичанин" (yà anglichanin)= I am English (male)

If you analyze the single words taken literally, you will notice something interesting:
Я = I
англичанин = English

...so, where is the verb "to be"??

5.1. An extinguished verb: to be or not to be?

The Russian verb "to be" in the present tense does not exist. Obviously in old Russian there were all the forms, but with the linguistic evolution they gradually extinguished. Nowadays, Russian students are lucky because they are not forced to learn by heart the conjugation "I am, you are, he/she/it is...!" How to build a sentence without the verb "to be"? The fact that the sentence lacks the verb does not mean that it is illogical: in the example at the beginning of the chapter the two words follows the same order that they would have in English.

Я (there is no verb) англичанин = I (am) English

For what concern this sentence order, Russian is really concise: let's see other examples.

singular:
Я студент (yà studiént) = I am a student (remember that in Russian there are no articles!)
Ты русский (ty rùsskij) = you are Russian
Он папа (on pàpa) = he is dad
Она мама (anà màma) = she is mom
Оно письмо = it is a letter (anò pismò; оно, "anò" is the third person singular of the neuter gender)

plural:
Мы подруги (my padrùghì) = we are friends (female friends)
Вы коллеги (vy kalliéghi) = you are colleagues
Они англичане (anì anglichanie) = they are English

As you can notice the verb "to be" is missing inside the sentence but it has a logical meaning anyway.

You can also find sentences like this one:
Иван – студент (Ivàn studiént) = Ivan is a student
Таня – мама (Tània màma) = Tanya is a mom

In these cases there is a graphic symbol meaning that in that point there is the verb "to be". This happens when the two words are both nouns (proper or common) and not a pronoun and a noun as we have already seen in the other sentences.
The hyphen, "tirè", is a sign that there is a verb "to be" in the sentences in which it could be forgotten.

Moreover, you have to know that only two forms of the old verb "to be" have survived the extinction, and just one of them is actively used in the modern Russian language: we are talking about the third singular person **есть**"iést"" (do not confuse it with the infinitive of the verb "to eat", written and pronounced all the same!). It could be translated as "to be" as well as "there is", and it is used in several phrases. We are going to pursue a very useful one in part 5.2.
ex. Хлеб **есть**? Есть. (Chliébiést'? ést') = is there some bread? Yes (there is).

In conclusion let's see how to build an interrogative and a negative sentence:
Я **не** русский, я англичанин. (yà nié rùsskij, yà anglichanin) = I am not Russian, I am English.
Ты русский? Нет. (Ty rùsskij? Niét) = are you Russian? No.

In this case too the Russian language proves to be very concise and clear: to deny something you just have to add the particle "не" (nié, do not) in the place of the verb "to be"; to ask for something you just have to use an interrogative tone (we will see this in lesson 7).

Remember: these rules focused on the negative and interrogative sentences are the same for all verbs!

5.2. The curious case of the verb "to have"

If the verb "to be" surprised you being easy to use, for you today is a day full of surprises: using the verb "to have" is easier than what you think it is. As always, let's try to understand it starting from an example:

У меня есть брат (U minyà iést' brat")

You already know almost all the words in this sentence:
У = "u" is a preposition of place, it means "at, by"
меня = "minyà" , it is the declined form of the pronoun "я"; we could translate it as "me"
есть = "iést", do you remember the surviving form of the verb "to be"? Here it is! Here it means "there is".
брат = a brother

So here it is our sentence translated literally:
"By me there is a brother" = I have a brother

If it looks like a little complicated, consider its advantages:
1. its structure does not change
2. here the direct object becomes subject
3. you will never have to decline the owned thing.

To know deeply the last point, I will have to explain somemore things about Russian language, but now there is no need to hurry! Let's see some examples of things you may have with you everyday, so that you can say it in Russian:

У меня есть книга U minià iést' knìga = I have a book
У меня есть друг U minià iést' drug = I have a friend
У меня есть собака U minià iést' sabàka = I have a dog
У меня есть сестра U minià iést' sistrà = I have a sister

Clearly, this alternative verb can be used also with the other persons:

У меня есть	U minià iést'	I have
У тебя есть	U tibià iést'	you have
У него / неё есть	U nievó / nieió iést'	he / she has
У нас есть	U nas iést'	we have
У вас есть	U vas iést'	you have
У них есть	U nich iést'	they have

The rule is always the same: U + personal pronoun + the owned thing

The personal pronoun in this sentence is declined, but we will see what it means in the next chapter. For now you just need to know these two structures so that you can understand the difference between what we are and what we have. Here the verbs "to be" and "to have" served in a single course in Russian sauce!

Let's disclose the secrets of this chapter

. The verb "to be" in Russian is nearly completely extinguished. In a sentence with the verb "to be", this is simply absent: я русский (ià rùsskij) = I am Russian. The same thing happens with all the persons.

. If the subject is a noun (common or proper) in the written form the verb "to be" is replaced by a hyphen called "tiré". It is the same in the speech form: you can hear a brief pause in the place of the verb "to be".

. For the negative form it is sufficient to add the negation "не" (nié) in the position of the missing verb.

. The only surviving form of the verb "to be" is есть (iést'), meaning "there is".

. Есть is also used to form the verb "to have", but it is not a proper verb, it is just a construction: у меня есть (u minià iést') = (literally) by me there is = I have

. This construction is used with all persons: the subject is always introduced by the preposition "у" (u) and it is declined in genitive case.

DAY 6: IN CASE...

Russians are really attached to the concept of "case" , interpreted as fate or destiny. Today, though, we are talking about a different kind of case: the grammatical case. Moving in this territory is like walking on quicksands: it is better knowing an expert guide and knowing the firm points to lean on. Obviously we cannot deal with this argument in this few pages due to its complexity, so we will keep studying it in the next chapters: you will definitively see the the sentence " in this case we are using the singular dative".

Just hearing "case", the bell of the respondent conditioning will probably ring in your head like it did with the dog looking for food in the Pavlovian experiment: in this situation, though, (unfortunately!) you will hear the grammar bell.

Let's see how to deal with this argument right away!

6.1. The cases of life (in Russia)

So, what is a case? A case is a grammatical category that modifies a noun depending on its logical function in the sentence. In English we do not decline nouns and adjectives in cases, but prepositions undergo the same function too. We have something similar too, in particular with the pronouns:

for example, "I, you, he /she / it / are personal pronouns subject, but in the sentence they can change in "me, you, him / her/ it…" if they are considered as direct object.

In Russian these two systems are used in parallel: there are prepositions but also- and especially- cases. Here the main logical functions of the Russian cases:

Nominative→ who? what? → subject
Genitive→ of whom? of what? → complement that specifies to whom or of whom
Dative→ to whom? to what? → indirect object
Accusative → who? what? → direct object
Instrumental case→ with who? with what? how? by what means? → it specifies the means of an action, with whom an action is done, when the action is done
Prepositional→ about who? about what? → it specifies the object of speech or thought (and others)

Unfortunately cases have not an univocal meaning: for example the instrumental case can specify also the predicative object of the subject (I will be a doctor = я буду врачом, yà bùdu vraciòm),or the prepositional has many different uses in the language.

Speaking a declined language could seem something we are forced to do, an eternal effort to "remember the rule", and you may think that these kind of languages are made of long and complex structures. Well, actually it is not like that: a first great advantage of cases is that thanks to them we can really synthesize the words used in a sentence.

For example:
ENG – I give mom a friend's present.
RUS – Я даю маме подарок подруги.(yà daiù màmie padàrak padrùghi)

As you can see, in the Russian sentence some words "disappear":
- articles: do you remember? In Russian they do not exist!
- prepositions: their grammatical role is carried out by cases

So, that word acquires a different role in the sentence depending on its last letter: маме= mom (to the mom, dative); подруги= friend's (genitive).

Did you notice how concise is the Russian sentence? This means more than it could seem at the beginning: do you know the masterpieces of Russian literature? They are not famous for being short novels. Some people give up the reading due to their apparent heaviness. Now that you know how the internal mechanisms of the Russian sentence works, you can start to approach those huge books more positively: after all, they have not been conceived as "real loads"!

The beauty of Russian is also in these little internal contradictions: a difficult method to obtain an easy and concise result aimed to communicate directly.
Another undeniable advantage of cases is in the construction of the sentence: where it is possible, we can say that the word order is not as important as it is in English. If the

words have their own grammatical essence, linking them to prepositions following a precise order is not necessary.

Lastly, if this concept is too difficult to you, think about the fact that children too learn cases at school! So, there are different sentences-nursery rhymes to learn by heart the cases order and their name in Russian, and the one I was taught goes like:

Иван Родил Девчонку, Велел Тащить Пелёнку
Ivàn radìl dievciònku, viéliel tashìt' pieliònku

and it means: "Ivan had a baby girl, now he has to change nappies".

The sentence itself does not make much sense, but it is useful to Russian children to learn by heart the names of the cases more easily. The initials of each word correspond to the initials of the names of the cases:

Иван - именительный - nominative
Родил - родительный - genitive
Девчонку - дательный - dative
Велел - винительный - accusative
Тащить - творительный - instrumental
Пелёнку - предложный - prepositional

6.2. The final part is fundamental

The cases are six and they distinguish themselves depending on the singular and plural, the hard and soft words and the three genders, maculine, feminine and neuter.
I know, it seems a lot of notions, but don't worry: I will explain everything more clearly in the next paragraph.

Let's get into the thick of the argument* and let's see the declension of some words:

- masculine: стол and конь (stol, table, kogn, horse);
- neuter: село and море (sielò, village, mòrie, sea).
- feminine: мама and тётя (màma, mom, tiòtia, aunt);

Tab. 3: DECLENSION OF NOUNS IN THE SINGULAR

gender	case	hard			soft		
M	Nom	стол	stol	the table	конь	kogn	horse
	Gen	стола	stalà	of the table	коня	kagnià	of the horse
	Dat	столу	stalù	to the table	коню	kagniù	to the horse
	Acc	стол	stol	the table (dir.obj)	коня*	kagnià	the horse (dir.obj)
	Instrum	столом	stalòm	with the table	конём	kagniàm	with the horse
	Prep	столе	stalie	(on) the table	коне	kagnié	(on) the horse
N	Nom	село	sielò	the village	море	mòrie	the sea
	Gen	села	sielà	of the village	моря	mòria	of the sea
	Dat	селу	sielù	to the village	морю	mòriu	to the sea
	Acc	село	sielò	the village (dir.obj)	море	mòrie	the sea (dir.obj)
	Instrum	селом	sielòm	with the village	морём	mariòm	with the sea
	Prep	селе	sielie	(in) the village	море	mòrie	(in) the sea
F	Nom	мама	màma	mom	тётя	tiòtia	the aunt
	Gen	мамы	màmy	mom's (Eng. Possessive)	тёти	tiòti	aunt's (Eng. Possessive)
	Dat	маме	màmie	to mom	тёте	tiòtie	to the aunt
	Acc	маму	màmu	mom (dir.obj)	тётю	tiòtiu	the aunt (dir.obj)
	Instrum	мамой	màmai	with mom	тётей	tiòtiei	with the aunt
	Prep	маме	màmie	(about) mom	тёте	tiòtie	(about) the aunt

Did you notice that suffixes in the masculine and neuter are the same? This make things easier! As a matter of fact, in Russian the neuter nouns are closer to the masculine ones than the feminine ones from a grammatical point of view, and for this reason they act as such in most cases.

Some clarifications about Table 3:

1. Take a look at the asterisk on the singular accusative of конь,кон**я*** (kagnyà, the horse) This happens because the accusative is a particular case: when the noun is inanimate (objects and abstarct thoughts) accusative and nominative are alike → ex. стол (stol)
When the noun is animated (people or animals), the accusative is identical to the genitive, like конь,кон**я**.

2. The last case, the prepositional, is always accompanied by a preposition, for this reason I added it in brackets. The typical prepositions that you can find with this case are о, на, в (o, na, v), meaning "about", "on", "in".

3. This apparently complicated scheme is actually based on concepts that we already know: the concepts of masculine, feminine and neuter (see chapter 4) and the difference between hard and soft vowels (see chapter 2). You just have to remember the hard declension to guess the soft one: стол**а** (hard), кон**я** (soft).

The cases are never enough: the plural follows the same scheme, but with different suffixes.

Tab. 4: DECLENSION OF NOUNS IN THE PLURAL

gender	case	hard			soft		
M	Nom	Столы	stalì	the tables	Кони	kagnì	the horses
	Gen	Столов	stalòv	of the tables	Коней	kagnièi	of the horses
	Dat	Столам	stalàm	to the tables	Коням	kagniàm	to the horses
	Acc	Столы	stalì	the tables (dir.obj.)	Коней*	kagnièi	the horses (dir.obj)
	Instrum	Столами	stalàmi	with the tables	Конями	kagniàmi	with the horses
	Prep	Столах	stalàkh	(on) the tables	Конях	kagniakh	(on) the horses
N	Nom	Сёла	siòla	the villages	Моря	marià	the seas
	Gen	Сёл	siòl	of the villages	Морей	marièi	of the seas
	Dat	Сёлам	siòlam	to the villages	Морям	mariàm	to the seas
	Acc	Сёла	siòla	the villages (dir.obj)	Моря	marià	the seas (dir.obj)
	Instrum	Сёлами	siòlami	with the villages	Морями	mariàmi	with the seas
	Prep	Сёлах	siòlakh	(in) the villages	Морях	mariàkh	(in) the seas
F	Nom	Мамы	màmy	the moms	Тёти	tiòti	the aunts
	Gen	Мам	mam.	moms'	Тёть*	tiòt'	aunts'
	Dat	Мамам	màmama	to the moms	Тётям	tiòtiam	to the aunts
	Acc	мам*	mam.	the moms (dir.obj)	тёть*	tiòt'	the aunts (dir.obj)
	Instrum	мамами	màmami.	with the moms	тётями	tiòtiami	with the aunts
	Prep	мамах	màmakh	(about) the moms	тётях	tiòtiakh	(about) the aunts

We won't focus so deeply on the nouns in the plural since I do not want to immerse you in too much work. You can always refer to this scheme if you are having doubts. The rules of this table are the same of the previous one: pay particular attention to the plural genitive, since it has a lot of different structures.

You will find these tables and the next ones at the ned of the textbook.

EXERCISE 5

Try identifying the gender of the words in brackets and decline them in the correct case making references to the tables 3 and 4. (answers and translation at the end of the chapter).

Genitive:

У _____ (сестра) есть дом.
u...iest' dom.

Это книга _____ (учитель).
èta knìga ...

Дайте мне литр _____ (молоко).
dàitie mnié litr ...

Я из _____ (Новгород)
yà is ...

Dative:

Я даю _____ (папа) зонтик.
yà daiù ... sòntik

Я звоню _____ (друг).
yà svaniù ...

Мы дарили цветы _____ (бабушка).
my darìli zvietì ...

Accusative:
Я вожу _____ (машина).
yà vajù ...

84

Ирина видела _____ (муж – il marito)
Irina vìdiela …

Мы слушаем _____ (музыка).
my slùshaiem …

Вася покупает _____ (яблоко)
Vàsia pakupàiet …

Instrumental:

Вы рисуете _____ (карандаш).
vy risùietie …

Я ела суп _____ (ложка).
yà iéla sup …

Иван работает _____ (кассир).
Ivan rabòtaiet …

Мы с _____ (подруга) идём в театре.
my s … idiòm v tieàtrie

Prepositional: (always used with a preposition)

Летом я отдыхаю<u>на</u> _____ (море)<
liétam yà addykhàiu na…

Маша сидит <u>на</u> _____ (диван)
Masha sidìt na …

Ты думаешь <u>об</u> _____ (экзамен)
ty dùmaiésh ab …

Вы говорите о _____ (жизнь — soft declension!)

vy gavarìtie a …

6.3. Don't choose at random!

In Russian you have to decline everything: nouns, pronouns, adjectives, participles, proper names of people and places, and last names too. The only parts of the sentence that never change are the adverbs, the prepositions and the particles, short words consisting in a few letters that will definitely help you when you will feel lost.
You cannot escape this linguistic mechanism, so it is better to face it openly, bearing in mind some little tricks:

- when you speak and you have doubts about the case of a word, you can "soften" its ending by pronunciating it not too clearly: your interlocutor will understand what you are talking about even if you do not articulate perfectly the whole word (or he/she will make an effort);

- what language would it be without irregular cases? You will find a lot of them in Russian. The trick is replacing the sentence with a synonym or a different construction. Example? Мама is an affectionate version of мать (mat', mother). This is an irregular term, so it is annoying, we can easily use its synonym since its meaning is identical;

- you will learn that some prepositions and verbs are matched with a specific case. By repeating them so much you will learn the construction automatically.

We have already seen something about this in the previous chapters, remember?

Let's recap:
<u>Меня</u> зовут… minyà zavùt … → singular accusative of the personal pronoun Я (yà = io).

Я из <u>Рим**а**</u>. Yà is Rìma → singular genitive of the proper noun Рим (Rim = Rome).

У<u>тебя</u> есть сестра. U tibià iést' siestrà → singular genitive of the personal pronoun ты (ty = you), governed by the preposition У (u = by).

The genitive is one of the most employed cases in the basic construction of the Russian language.

In the next chapters as we keep going with the study of cases, I will point out in bold the ending of the words explaining what case it is in brackets.

EXERCISE 6

Take a look at this short text and the cases that I highlighted:

Добрый мальчик – A good boy
Папа (*Nom*) и сын (*Nom*) были в магазине (*Prep*).
Мальчик (*Nom*) увидел барабан (*Acc*) и сказал папе (*Dat*):
"Папа (*Nom*), купи мне, пожалуйста, этот красный
барабан (*Acc*). Я буду на нём играть, он очень красивый!".
"Нет, не куплю, - ответил папа (*Nom*). - Когда я буду
работать, ты будешь играть **на** барабане (*Prep*) и мешать
мне". "Папочка (*Nom*), я буду играть на нём, когда ты
будешь спать!"

pronunciation:
Pàpa i syn byli v magazìnie.
Màl'chik uvìdiel baràbàn i skasàl pàpie: "Pàpa, kupì mnié, pajàlusta, ètat baràbàn. yà bùdu na niòm igràt', on òcien' krasìvyi!". "Niét, nié kupliù, - atviétil pàpa. – Kagdà ià bùdu rabòtat', ty bùdiesh igràt' na baràbàne i mieshàt' mnié". "Pàpa-
chka, yà bùdu igràt' na niòm, kagdà ty bùdiesh spat'!"

translation:
A dad and his son are in a shop.
The kid sees a drum and he asks his dad: "Dad, please, buy
me that red drum. I will play it, it is so nice!"
"No, I won't buy it, - his dad answers. –When I will be
working, you will play the drum and it will be annoying".
"Daddy, I will play it when you will be working then!"

Pay attention: the original text is in the past tense, but I
translated in the present tense so that it is easier.

Now, try to do the same with this second text: find the cases for each noun (the answers at the end of the chapter). If you need help you can take a look at the translation:

Я <u>студентка</u>, учусь в<u>университете</u>. Я из <u>Америки</u>. Сейчас я изучаю только русский <u>язык</u>, а потом буду учиться **на** <u>факультете</u> журналистики. Хочу стать <u>журналисткой</u>. Я интересуюсь русской <u>историей</u>, <u>литературой</u>. Сейчас у меня мало <u>практики</u> русского <u>языка</u>: поэтому, я решила больше говорить **на** <u>улице</u> и **в** <u>магазине</u>.

pronunciation:
yà studiéntka, uchùs' v universitiétie. yà is Amiériki Sichas' yà isuchàiu tòl'ka rùsski yasìk, a patòm bùdu ucìzza na fakul'tiétie jurnalìstiki. Khaciù stat' jurnalìstkai. Yà intieriesùius' rùsskai istòriei, litieratùrai. Sichas' u minià màla pràktiki rùsskava yasikà: paètamu yà rieshìla bòl'she gavarìt' na ùlize i v magasìnie.

translation:
I am a university student. I come from the United States. Right now I just study Russian language but in the future I am going to study journalism. I want to become a journalist. I am interested in Russian history and literature. Right now I am not so experienced with the Russian language: so I decided to practice it outside and in shops.

Let's disclose the secrets of this chapter

. Russian is a language that has cases: a noun indicates its logical function in the sentence thanks to its ending suffix.

. The Russian language has six cases. They are valid for the three genders (masculine, neuter and feminine) and for each case they have two forms: hard and soft suffix. This rule is the same for the plural.

. Sometimes the cases can be accompanied by a preposition, short words that never change in the sentence. For example, the prepositional is always accompanied by a preposition.

. The suffixes of masculine and neuter are almost identical. Two for the price of one!

. In Russian almost every part of the speech is declined: proper and common nouns, adjectives, pronouns and participles.

. To avoid complicated constructions with cases try turning the sentence over or using synonyms!

ANSWERS.

Exercise 5

Genitive:
сестры — The sister has a house
учителя — This book belongs to the teacher.
молока — Give me a liter of milk (formal)
Новгорода — I come from Novgorod

Dative:
папе — I give dad an umbrella
другу — I make a call to a friend
бабушке — We gave flowers to grandma

Accusative:
машину — I drive the car
мужа — Irina saw her husband
музыку — We listen to the music
яблоко — Vasya buys an apple

Instrumental:
карандашом — You draw with a pencil
ложкой — I ate soup with a spoon
кассиром — Ivan works as a cashier
подругой — I go to the theater with a friend

Prepositional:
на море — During summer I spend the holidays at the sea
на диване — Masha is laying on the sofa
об экзамене — You think about the exam
о жизни — You talk about life

EXERCISE 6

студентка = feminine nominative

в университете = masculine prepositional

из Америки = feminine genitive governed by the preposition **из**

язык = masculine accusative (identical to the nominative for inanimated objects)

на факультете = masculine prepositional governed by the preposition **на**

журналистики = feminine genitive

журналисткой = feminine instrumental, always used with the verb стать, to become

историей, литературой = feminine instrumental, always with the verb интересоваться, being interested in something

мало практики = feminine genitive, because it is governed by the adverb мало, "a little bit of"

русского языка = masculine genitive

на улице = feminine prepositional governed by the preposition **на**

в магазине = masculine prepositional governed by the preposition **в**

DAY 7: FIRST STEPS IN RUSSIA

Dear reader, today we are going to use again the language in a practical way. Obviously, we take for granted that a trip to Russia is inevitable soon or later!
So, here some daily situation where you can actively put into practice what you have learned until now.

7.1. Airport: shock therapy

There is nothing better than a take-off toward a new destination! The thrill, the feeling of a new adventure… Getting to Russia for the first time means, in most cases, getting to an airport. This is where a real shock therapy with the Russian language begins: you will suddenly be immersed in an infinite bunch of words written in Cyrillic, and you will also hear dialogues in Russian. There is no better place to begin the practice of a language.

First of all, the alphabet: it is important to become immediately familiar with this different writing system, not to understand exactly every sign but rather to have the certainty of your ability in reading.

Luckily, international airports often uses English too in signs; do not get used to it, though: once outside, you won't use English so much.

For how banal it may seems, in Russia you will get by especially by using Russian: becoming familiar with the language right away is extremely important.

7.2. Brief daily survival course

There are some essential words that cannot be missed in your linguistic experience, not only to pronounce them but also to understand what they mean when you see or hear them.

In the chapter focused on greetings we have seen the main forms of courtesy and how to use them. Let's move forward and let's concentrate on daily situations:

<u>Entry or exit: pull/push</u>
Вход / выход: two apparently identical words that diversify for a single letter. You find this sign on doors and it is important to distinguish the meaning:

Вход (vchod) is the entry; **выход** (východ) is the exit. For this reason, a lot of words are matched in couples with opposite meanings showing these two different prefixes:

в- (v) = inside
вы- (vy) = outside

In Russian, the prefixes are useful clues to understand the meaning of a word. Some of them, such as **в**, work as unique prepositions:

ex.   я в России – yà v Rassìi – I am in Russia (России is a singular feminine *prepositional*)

ты в аэропорту – ty v aerapartù – you are in airport (аэропорту is singular masculine *irregular* prepositional)

The structure "**в** + *prepositional*" indicates the place.
Another expression containing prepositions, that you can find on doors, is the corresponding translation of

"pull/push": even in Russia it is better to avoid pulling doors instead of pushing them and for this reason remember that

на себя (na sibyà) = towards you, "pull"
от себя (ot sibyà) = away from you, "push"
In this case **на** and **от** are not prefixes but prepositions.

I need...
Ask and you will be given. As long as you ask correctly, otherwise people might not understand you. In Russian there are different ways to express need, and here the use of the pronouns in dative case is fundamental:

мне надо– mnié nàda
мне нужно – mnié nùjna
мне необходимо – mnié nieabchadìma

In general, they all mean "I need", but the degree of need grows gradually:

мне надо – mnié nàda – I need
мне нужно – mnié nùjna – I need (necessarily)
мне необходимо – mnié nieabchadìma – it is necessary

This is another structure that, like the verb "to have", works with cases and this time with indeclinable adverbs (надо, нужно). The first word, in our case **мне** (mnié), to me, is the pronoun "I" (я) declined in *dative*.

Мне надо (mnié nàda) can be combined directly with nouns:
мне надо яблоко (mnié nàda iàblaka, I need an apple)

On the contrary the other two expressions undergo changes
depending on the following noun (the needed thing):
(мне) нужен + masculine noun   mnié nùjen
(мне) нужна + feminine noun   mnié nujnà
(мне) нужно + neuter noun

(мне)

Tab. 5: PERSONAL PRONOUNS IN NOMINATIVE, GENITIVE AND DATIVE

	nominative		genitive		dative	
I- me- to me	Я	Yà	Меня	minyà	Мне	mniè
You- you- to you	Ты	ty	Тебя	tibyà	Тебе	tibiè
He- him- to him	Он	on	(н)его	n-ievò	Ему	iemù
She- her- to her	Она	anà	(н)её	n-ieiò	Eй	ièi
It- it- to it	Оно	anò	(н)его	n-ievò	Ему	iemù
We- us - to us	Мы	my	Нас	nas	Нам	nam
You- you- to you	Вы	vy	Вас	vas	Вам	vam
They- them - to them	Они	ani	(н)их	n-ich	Им	im

With this table we recap all forms of pronouns that we have studied until now. The nominative for the verb "to be", the genitive for the construction of possession and the dative for the constuction of "need".
Now, let's see how to use this new expression.

Reference points:
In Russia there are particular and essential places for the daily survival of a stranger :

supermarket: супермаркет - supermàrkiet

subway: метро - mietrò
restaurant: ресторан - riestaràn
bank: банк - bank
ticket booth: билетная касса - biliétnaya kàssa

And also, in extremely necessary situations:

pharmacy: аптека - aptiéka
embassy: посольство - pasòlstva
hospital: больница - bal'nìza
police: полиция - palìzia

So, if you ever need a bank, you just have to say "мне надо банк", mnié nàda bank, I need a bank.

EXERCISE 7

Let's try to make a few sentences: for each use the simple form мне надо or нужно that changes depending on the gender.

ex. I need a supermarket: мне надо супермаркет / мне нужен супермаркет
(mnié nàda supermàrkiet / mnié nùjen supermàrkiet)

1) I need a restaurant.
2) You need a pharmacy.
3) We need a station.
4) He needs the subway.
5) You need a hospital.
6) They need the embassy and the police.
7) She needs a ticket booth.

As always the answers are at the end of the chapter.

7.3. Don't speak to me in that tone of voice!

Lastly,an important topic is the intonation. Learning the tone could seem unnecessary since, for now, you just know short phrases and a few grammatical constructions, but it is really useful above all to understand what a Russian is trying to tell you. A good part of the cultural conceptions that we create about a people derives from the sound of their language and from the feeling that we confer to it: so, the French people are all romantic, Germans strike fear, Spaniards are *calientes* and Russians… What about Russians? Inevitably they sound "cold", maybe unfriendly and not so particularly willing towards us. Well, it takes nothing to realize though, that these "phonetic prejudices" are absolutely unfounded: it is true that every language has its own sound, but this does not determine the temper of the speaker!

If you want to know better the sensation of the sound of the Russian language, you have to know the system behind it: we have already studied the main phonetic rules, the existence of hard and soft sounds, and also the seriousness of Russians when it comes to smile with no reason to anyone in the street.

So, it is time to add an important theme, the **intonation**. We are not used to study this aspect in the most common European languages. A classic example is the question tone: when we study the different constructions in English, French or German, we do not consider the tone of that question: we understand it from the structure of the sentence or we deduce it from the question tone.

Russian is different because it has a precise intonation scheme depending on the type of sentence. There are 7 intonations (интонационные коиструкции, intanaziònnye kanstrùkzii, generally abbreviated with ИК), but it is just a classification created to simplify the study to a foreign speaker: actually, as always, the language is faster than

grammar and not all sentences can be classified in this scheme.
Let's see a few examples to understand the differences with our language:

ex. 1 – <u>declarative sentence</u> Это моя мама (èta mayà màma = this is my mom).
The intonation 1 (ИК-1) Это моя мама (èta mayà màma = it produces a "flat" sentence in which the tone falls at the end.

```
-    -    \
```
это моя **мама**

In Russian all declarative sentences (affirmative and negative) end with a dropping tone that do not go back up. This a first difference that points out the apparently "serious" tone of the Russians when they speak. It could seem a pedantic tone, but it is actually neuter and it is used normally to speak. It is also important to know that the word marked by the tone contains the most important information: take a look at the differences

```
-        \        -
```
это **моя** мама = This is my mom (mine, not yours)

```
\       -       -
```
это моя мама = This is my mom (This one, not that one)
The intonation is a really helpful tool to distinguish the essential information of the sentence that the Russian speaker wants to point out.
This system based on the tone "switch" on a word rather than another, is valid for all intonation schemes: if it seems a lot distant from our language, think that in English we often speak emphasizing a concept with pauses, or articulating or

raising our tone. In Russian this happens by switching intonation.

ex. 2 – question introduced by adverbs: Где ваша собака? (Gdié vàsha sabàka? Where is your dog?)
Here the tone of the voice slightly changes as compared to ИК-1 because, even if it drops, it is higher and more decisive: after all, it is a question and you absolutely want to know the answer! Here the three variants of the example sentence:

\\   -   -
Где ваша собака? = **Where** is your dog?

-        \\   -
Где ваша собака? = Where is **your** dog? (I perfectly know where mine is)

-       -   \\
Где ваша собака? = Where is your **dog**? (I saw the cat, but the dog is missing!)

The presence of a question mark should not mislead you, it does not mean that the tone has to be higher at the end. In Russian, if the question is introduced by an interrogative adverb (where, how, when, why etc…) the tone will always be flat, pointing out though the most important word (generally the interrogative adverb itself).

Studying the intonations on textbooks I have always thought: "Well it cannot be so difficult: I am sure that speaking I will understand without taking care of the intonation so precisely!".

I changed my mind while I was doing my grocery shop during an evening in Saint-Petersburg. I saw a shop assistant carrying a long row of shop carts (тележка, tieliéjka) and my friend Sabina and I asked in Russian if we could take one . The shop assistant was a little perplexed when he heard our question: probably our Russian version of "can we take a shop cart?"sounded like a happy new year wish or something like that, with toasts and celebration. Well, in that moment all my certainties about the uselessness of intonations fell apart in a second. I reflected for a moment and then I asked the same question with the correct intonation and miraculously I obtained my shop cart.

Maybe the shop assistant was going through a bad day or maybe he did not understand if we were actually asking him a question. The point is that this simple episode proved that intonations are fundamental if you want to be correctly understood!

Tab. 6: 7 INTONATIONS AND THEIR USE

ИК-1 declarative sentences:

Это моя мама

ИК-2 interrogative sentences introduced by adverbs:

Где ваша собака?

ИК-3 generic interrogative sentences:

(the tone goes upt and then becomes flat again)

У тебя есть ручка? = do you have a pen?

ИК-4 interrogative sentences that point out a comparison:
(the tone is higher than the 3)

А ты? = and you?

ИК-5 interjections introduced by "как / какой" (=what):

Какая погода! = what a wonderful weather!

ИК-6 enthusiasm interjection: (the tone goes up and it stays high)

Как весело! = that's wonderful!

ИК-7 ironic-derogatory interjection:

Какие они друзья! = what friends!

107

Let's disclose the secrets of this chapter

. When you get to Russia for the first time, take advantage of every kind of place you find yourself in: the airport is a great gym where you can practice the language.

. In the daily life there are expressions that cannot be missing in you linguistic experience. You have to link a grammatical theme to the active use of the language, so that it is easier to remember the rule.

. The sentence to express "I need" helps you remember the use of the dative inside the sentence: personal pronoun in dative + expression of necessity (adverbs надо or нужно declined) + what you need.

. The sentence with надо (nàda) is easier; on the contrary нужно (nùjna) must be declined in the same gender or number of the following word: M нужен – nùjen, F нужна – nujnà, N нужно – nùjna; Plural нужны – nujný.

. In a new place, you better have some reference points easy to recognize: in this chapter I point out the most immediate and fundamental ones.

. The Russian language uses different kind of intonation depending on the type of sentence. It is important to distinguish the tone differences between English and Russian, above all in the questions.

ANSWERS.

Exercise 7

1) I need a restaurant. – Мне надо ресторан / мне нужен ресторан

2) You need a pharmacy. – Тебе надо аптека / Тебе нужна аптека

3) We need a station. – Нам надо вокзал / нам нужен вокзал

4) He needs the subway. – Ему надо метро / Ему нужно метро

5) You need a hospital. – Вам надо больница / Вам нужна больница

6) They need the embassy and the police. – Им надо посольство и полиция / Им нужны посольство и полиция

7) She needs a ticket booth. – Ей надо билетная касса / ей нужна билетная касса

DAY 8: A CHARACTER MATTER

Today we are moving forward into the Russian communication: until now, you have learned how to read and pronunciate the most difficult sounds, how to have a basic conversation based on greetings and general pleasantries; you have studied the strangeness of the verbs "to be" and "to have" and you have also learned the use of three of the cases of the Russian language.

In this chapter we are going to focus on how to express our opinion about someone or something by using adjectives.

8.1. How to describe qualities

Let's begin with the qualifying adjectives: where do we place them inside the sentence? And how do they work grammatically? For example:

Ты **хороший** друг – Ty charòscii drug – You (are) a good friend

У меня есть **красивая** сестра – U minyà iést' krasìvaya siestrà – I have a beautiful sister

As you can see, the adjective is always before the noun. This happens for a simple reason: take a look what happens if we invert them

Друг **хороший**– Drug charòscii – The friend <u>is</u> good
Сестра **красивая** – Sistrà krasìvaya – The sister <u>is</u> beautiful

If the adjective follows the noun, it becomes the nominal part of the verb "to be", that, as you already know, does not appear in the sentence!

So, first rule to keep in mind: the qualifying adjective is always placed before the noun it refers to.

But how do we recognize an adjective in the sentence?

We can distinguish these words from nouns by observing their final part:

1) the masculine adjective ends with ый – ой / ий
2) the feminine adjective ends with ая / яя
3) the neuter adjective ends with oe / ee

Clearly this method is valid just for the nominative: at the end of the chapter you will find a table for the adjective declension that is really similar to the noun scheme that we have studied at chapter 6.

Here a few useful pairs of adjectives with the examples: I recommend studying them paired, so that you can memorize them both and it could come in handy if you wanted to turn the sentence over denying an adjective rather than using the contrary.

Большой / маленький   bal'shòi / màlien'kii
(big / small)

Do you know the famous Bolshoj Theater? It is the "big" theater of Moscow. Nearby you can also find the Малый Театр (Màlyi Tiàtr), "small theater". Малый is another version of the more common маленький.

Старый / Новый   stàryi / nòvyi
(old / new)

This pair of adjectives is really common in a lot of expressions: the most obvious example is the New Year's Eve, in Russian Старый Новый Год, Stàryi Nòvyi God, literally "Old New Year": it is a unique moment in which two years meet, and Russians love to remember both.

Высокий / Низкий   visòkii / nìskii
(tall-high / short-low)

These adjectives are used to express the stature of a person but also heights in general. Moreover, common adverbs derive from these adjectives, such as выше / ниже, vìshe / nìje, "above / below".

Хороший / плохой   charòshii / plachòi
(good / bad)

You should recognize these words since we have already studied the corresponding adverbs when it comes to answer the question как дела? (kak dielà?), how are you?: хорошо or плохо.

Длинный / короткий
(long / short)

dlìnnyi / karòtkii

Широкий / узкий
(wide / narrow)

shiròkii / ùskii

These adjectives are perfect to describe a street: in the big Russian cities you can find every kind of street, from the tree-lined ones and длинные бульвары (bul'vàr, a Russian word with a french origin), to the more короткий and узкий переулок (pierieùlak, alley), passing through a широкий проспект (praspiékt, avenue) like the Nevskij in Saint-Petersburg. You have a lot of choice!

Лёгкий / трудный
(easy / difficult)

liòkki / trùdnyi

Focus on the different sound of these two adjectives: liòkki is lighter, like something that flies ("light" is another meaning); on the contrary trùdnyi calls to mind a metallic and puffing machine in production phase, so heavy in its activity. At first you could say русский язык трудный (rùsskii iasyk trùdnyi, Russian language is difficult). But in a few lessons everything will be liòkki.

Красивый / плохой - некрасивый
krasìvyi / plachòi – niekrasìvyi
(beautiful / ugly-bad – not beautiful)

I think this is one of the most beautiful adjective of Russian: for no other reason "krasìvyi" means "beautiful". In order to make its contrary we can use plachòi, as "ugly" (but also bad), or we can use a useful trick to avoid any kind of linguistic hindrance: we can deny the adjective with a little and simple **не-** at the beginning of the word, the same negation we need with verbs. In this way it is possible to soften the tone of the disapproval:

- What does your friend Ivan look like?

113

- A little **niekrasìvyi** bu he is funny!

A real character I'd say.

8.2. Adjectives put into practice

In Russian there are a lot of different adjectives, as it is in English. You will notice that learning them all in a few pages requires a long time (длинный) and it is also difficult (трудный); so, as we go forward toward new chapters we will add some useful notions. In this final part I want to focus the attention on a particular group of adjectives, the possessive ones, and also on grammatical aspects. Last but not least!

Possessive adjectives:
They have a slightly different structure in comparison with the previous ones:

Tab. 7: POSSESSIVE ADJECTIVES (NOMINATIVE CASE)

	M		F		N		PL	
my	Мой	mòi	Моя	mayà	Моё	mayò	Мои	mai
your	Твой	tvòi	Твоя	tvayà	Твоё	tvayò	Твои	tvai
his	Его	ievò	Его		его		его	
her	Её	ieyò	Её		её		её	
its	Его	ievò	Его		его		его	
our	Наш	nash	Наша	nasha	Наше	nashe	Наши	nàshi
your	Ваш	vash	Ваша	vasha	Ваше	vashe	Ваши	vàshi
their	Их	ich	Их		Их		Их	

In this table I included just the nominative case (the basic case of the subject), but for now, let's just focus on these adjectives: if some of them change in every gender and in the plural too, others – those in the third person in singular and plural stay unchanged. The difference with English is that here it is more important who owns something than the

115

owned thing itself. The distinctive trait of Russian is that even the adjective of the third person in plural,**их**, stays unchanged.

Adjectives in all cases:
Well, I know that the fact that you have to decline the adjectives too requires a great concentration when it comes to learn the new suffixes. You will see though, that these can be really useful when you have to remember how to decline a noun and vice versa.
This time in the table I will add just the suffixes in the various cases. As follows, we will see some examples:

Tab. 8: DECLENSION OF ADJECTIVES

Case	M soft/hard	F soft/hard	N soft/hard	PL soft/hard
Nominative	-ый or -ой/-ий	-ая/-яя	-ое/-ее	-ые/-ие
Genitive	-ого/-его	-ой/-ей	-ого/-его	-ых/-их
Dative	-ому/-ему	-ой/-ей	-ому/-ему	-ым/-им
Accusative	=Nom or Gen*	-ую/-юю	=Nom	=Nom or Gen*
Instrumental	-ым/-им	-ой/-ей	-ым/-им	-ыми/-ими
Prepositional	-ом/-ем	-ой/ей	-ом/-ем	-ых/-их

*= Nom. is the noun is inanimated; =Gen. if the noun is animated.

If "the beautiful mom" is the subject, then it is красив**ая** мам**а**; if it is direct object (accusative case) then it is красив**ую** маму.

If an old friend comes visit, then he is the subject of the sentence, so the nominative is м**ой** стар**ый** друг.

If I decide to make a present to my old friend I will use the dative (to him) and it is мо**ему** стар**ому** друг**у**.

116

Lastly, if I am speaking with difficult words (слово, slòva, singular nominative) they would say that I am expressing myself трудными словами.

These few examples are useful to make you understand how musicality is a part of phonetic phenomena: the fact that the adjective and the noun rhyme together when we decline them, helps memorizing more rapidly the grammatical rules.

EXERCISE 8

Let's try right away with a comprehension exercise: the answers are at the end of the chapter!
Ex. моей сестре = to my sister (FEM.SING.DAT)

1) длинные улицы (улица = street)
2) большому банку
3) хорошую аптеку
4) в маленьком театре
5) нового города (город = city)

EXERCISE 9

Take a look at the text and determine the case of the adjective highlighted. You can help yourself with the translation.

Новый студент

В нашей группе – новый студент. Его зовут Мохаммед. Он приехал из далекой теплой африканской страны Марокко. Он не знает русского языка, но свободно говорит по-арабски, хорошо по-французски и немного по-английски. У себя дома он учился в национальном университете на математическом факультете. Мохаммед хочет стать хорошим экономистом, знать много иностранных языков и работать в крупной фирме.

В нашей группе _____
новый студент _____
из далекой теплой африканской страны _____
не знает русского языка _____
в национальном университете _____
на математическом факультете _____
стать хорошим экономистом _____

118

много иностранных языков _____

в крупной фирме _____

In our group there is a new student. His name is Mohammed. He comes from a far and hot African country, Morocco. He does not know Russian language but he fluently speaks Arabic, he is good in French and he also speaks a bit of English. In his country he has studied at the national university in the mathematics department. Mohammed wants to become a good economist, to know a lot of foreign languages and to work in an important firm.

Let's disclose the secrets of this chapter

. The adjective precedes the noun as its qualifier.

. As the nouns, adjectives have three genders and each with the hard/soft forms.

. Often the adjectives have a contrary; if there is not one or if you want to deny the adjective in a "softer" way, you can put the prefix не- (nie-) at the beginning.

. It is worth studying the adjectives in pairs with their contraries: two for the price of one.

. The possessive adjectives are different: as a matter of fact the third person ones, both singular and plural are invariable. It is always essential to observe the gender of the possessor and not that of the owned thing: his/her – their.

. Declining nouns and adjectives together is not hard if you keep in mind their musicality, like in "rhymes".

ANSWERS.

Exercise 8

1) длинные улицы — dlìnnye ùlizzy — long streets (PLUR.FEM.NOM)

2) большому банку — bal'shòmu bànku — to the big bank (SING.MASC.DAT)

3) хорошую аптеку — charòshuiu aptiéku — the good pharmacy (SING.FEM.ACC)

4) в маленьком театре — v màlien'kam tiàtrie — in the small theater (SING.MASC.PREP.)

5) нового города — nòvava gòrada — of the new city (SING.MASC.GEN.)

Exercise 9

В нашей группе= singular feminine prepositional

новый студент = singular masculine nominative

из далекой теплой африканской страны = singular feminine genitive

(не знает) русского языка = singular masculine genitive

в национальном университете = singular masculine prepositional

на математическом факультете = singular masculine prepositional

(стать) хорошим экономистом= singular masculine instrumental

много иностранных языков = plural masculine genitive

в крупной фирме = singular feminine prepositional

DAY 9: SNOW AND OTHER ATMOSPHERIC PHENOMENA

Dear reader, today we are going to deal with one of my favourite themes, as well as one of the most common and great prejudices about Russia: the climate! As every kind of prejudice, the classic sentence "in Russia it's cold" is a kernel of truth. To be clear, this is a truth that lasts 8 months. You will surely learn that there are different types of cold, as in the remaining 4 months Russians enjoy different types of heat.

In this chapter we are going to deal with the different expressions to describe meteorological weather and the temperature. After all, the weather is a great topic to start a conversation with someone, right?

The city landscape is not so fairy, but I can assure you that it has its charm...

9.1. What a wonderful day!

I remember a car spot set in a rainy northern Europe, in which a man left every morning smiling and crying out *"What a wonderful day!"*. I would like you to have the same enthusiasm toward th Russian climate, something we are not used to. Russian winters are freezing and the more you move away from the city, the more you feel it. On the contrary, summers can be incredibly hot, almost 40 degrees (even if for a few joyful moments)!

Talking about the weather can be a simple way to start an informal conversation or an excuse when you do not know what to talk about. Moreover, to Russians, knowing your foreign point of view on weather could be really interesting. Let's see some useful sentence:

What's the weather like today? = Какая сегодня **погода?** (Kakàya sivòdnya pagòda?)

Погода (pagòda) is the keyword: this is the Russian word to refer to meteorological weather.

Снег идёт = sniég idiòt = it is snowing (literally "the snow goes")

As the snow, the rain can "go" too: **Идёт дождь** = idiòt dojd'

The wind blows: **ветер дует**, viétier dùiet (the wind blows)

The sun is a rare event during winter, but it is more frequent starting from the spring on: they say that it "shines"– **сольнце светит**, sònze sviétit.

Attention: "sun" (**сольнце**) is a neuter noun and it is a part of those words that have a group of consonants that are reduced in pronunciation: the "n" wins over the "l" reducing the pronunciation to "sonze".

Another useful sentence is that one to express if you are cold or hot: we have already seen this expression to state a "need", dative + adverb

мне холодно / жарко / тепло
mnié chòladna / jàrka / tieplò
I am cold / hot / warm

You could also hear a Russian saying "Skòl'ka gràdusov sivòdnia?"(сколько градусов сегодня?) and the answer could surprise you: before the number of the degrees they always specify "plus" or "minus" (pliùs – mìnus). From the context, guessing the temperature is obvious, but in spring saying that it is 10 degrees is not clear at all: +10° or -10°?

After all, you have to know that the Russian winter is rarely damp, so it is much more tolerable than the winter we are used to, although it is necessary to be ready to face it: you have to keep in mind that in winter, if outside the cold is cutting, inside the houses and pubs all over the city the heat is guaranteed, even too much! It is not a rare thing finding heated up floors that will melt the remaining snow on your shoes as well as will keep your feet warm. The balance between the two worlds is that, when you are tired of the heat, you can go outside in the cold, and when you are fed up with the cold, you can come back inside to warm up. In both cases, the sensation of change is always nice: winter evenings in Saint-Petersburg are made of struggles against snow and cold and also of long conversations over a cup of tea or coffe, to come back again in the storm to go home.
From our "temperate" point of view, Russia is a land of extremities.

What about the hot? Summer in cities are so hot that it is not rare seeing people swimming in rivers or in the city small lakes, the same ones that in winter lie down under a thick sheet of ice. In the most cold months of the year you can easily walk on them (you absolutely have to try once in your life!). The most bold citizens, when they are running late, cross the river or the frozen canals even by bike! Starting from March on, when the sun peeks out between the dense clouds, it is better not to risk. Let's let the Russians do these crazy things!

Russia is a country full of magic in every season you visit it: winter cannot live without summer and viceversa. The connection is much stronger than that we conceive with our four seasons, more or less defined.

9.2. Wuthering heights

This peculiarity of the climate affects the linguistic terminology. As the peoples living in the desert use different expressions to refer to sand, in the same way Russians use several terms to refer to snow and its phenomena:

крупа, krupà, is the mealy snow

фирн, firn (or firnòvyi sneg) is the "hard" frozen snow, that accumulates at the sides of the streets after a great snowfall

метель (mietiél') is the snow storm in which the wind strongly blows snowflakes;

позёмок (pasiòmak) is when the wind raises the snow laying on the ground, contributing to the worsening of visibility for drivers.

пурга(purgà – be careful to the accent!) is a synonym of **метель**, such as **буря** (bùria), that can also indicate a generic storm.

Lastly, **снежная мгла** (sniéjnaia mglà), snowy mist, it generally follows a snow storm.

So, the snowflakes are all different.
It is interesting noticing that the sun has not this great lexical variety: there is just one sun. And after all, Russians love thinking it in this way.

Let's disclose the secrets of this chapter

. In Russia the climate is always a "hot" topic.

. Every atmospheric phenomena is expressed in its own way: the snow and the rain "go", the wind "blows" and the sun "shines".

. In order to say "I am hot / cold" you have to use the same grammatical structure that we have studied to express "need": dative + adverb, ex. мне холодно. Attention! In these cases never use the verb "to have"! Remember that the verb "to have" is always for the possession. In this case we are talking about the sensations and not the objects that we own.

. When we talk about the temperature, we have always to specify if the degrees are plus or minus, above all in the intermediate seasons.

. In Russia cold and hot coexist in a necessary alternation.

. The snow can have different names depending on how it is and on how it falls.

DAY 10: LET'S MOVE INTO ACTION, HOW TO CONJUGATE VERBS

We cannot move forward just with the verbs "to be" and "to have", so today we are going to focus on the others. We are going to take a verb for each conjugation category as an example (first conjugation, second conjugation and then the irregular ones!). At the end of every paragraph I will point out a list of useful verbs that have the same type of conjugation.

10.1. How to distinguish a verb

Until now, we have talked about nouns and adjectives. We have dealt with the the verbs "to be" and "to have" too, but they are not helpful to make us understand how the other verbs work. Moreover, how do we distinguish a verb?

The infinitive of the majority of Russian verbs ends with **–ть**. There are different conjugations depending on the vowel preceding "**ть**" :

FIRST CONJUGATION: verbs that in the infinitive form end with -ать, -ять, -еть

SECOND CONJUGATION: verbs that in the infinitive form end with -ить, -еть, (rarely with ать too)

As you can see, "-еть" double-crosses a little: in some cases, the verbs in the infinitive form ending with it, are considered irregular. A double-cross at different levels. Don't worry, though: the first and second conjugation are not so different, so, if you are having doubts, you can always try one way or the other.

You can happen also to find reflexive verbs ending with the same scheme **vowel + ть** but with the reflexive suffix **ся** in addition:

ex. одеваться = одев – а – ть – ся
root – thematic vowel - suffix of the verb – reflexive suffix

Attention! There are also nouns ending with the group **ть**, a characteristic of the infinitive of verbs. You will be able to distinguish them once you become more familiar with the language. First thing to do is finding the verb when you read a Russian text. If you have doubts, refer to a dictionary.

If you want to look a verb up in the dictionary, it is necessary for you to know its infinitive, and if you want to distinguish a verb inside the sentence, you need to know its conjugated forms. Let's see them together in the next paragraph.

10.2. First and second conjugation verbs

The Russian verb has two conjugations: for the first one we will study the verb **читать** (citàt', to read), for the second one the verb **говорить** (gavarìt', to speak).

FIRST CONJUGATION
я ЧИТАЮ
ты ЧИТАЕШЬ
он ЧИТАЕТ
мы ЧИТАЕМ
вы ЧИТАЕТЕ
они ЧИТАЮТ

SECOND CONJUGATION
я ГОВОРЮ
ты ГОВОРИШЬ
он ГОВОРИТ
мы ГОВОРИМ
вы ГОВОРИТЕ
они ГОВОРЯТ

Take a look at the differences between the two conjugations:
- in the first one the thematic A of the infinitive does not change, but there is another vowel in addition (E / Ю depending on the number of the person)
- in the second one the vowel И of the infinitive has two functions and for "I" and "they" it disappears and it is replaced by the vowels of the suffixes.

With the exception of the vowel, as you can see, the final parts of the words do not change. So, we can say that if you want to conjugate a verb, you just have to remember these suffixes:

я – Ю / У
ты – (vowel) ШЬ
он – (vowel) Т
мы – (vowel) М
вы – (vowel) ТЕ
они – (vowel) Т

Lastly, some second conjugation verbs undergo a slight change in the first singular person: take a look at the conjugation of the verbs **любить** (liubìt', to love) and **видеть** (vìdiet', to see)

я ЛЮБ<u>Л</u>Ю, ты ЛЮБИШЬ, он ЛЮБИТ, мы ЛЮБИМ, вы ЛЮБИТЕ, они ЛЮБЯТ

яВИ<u>Ж</u>У, ты ВИДИШЬ, он ВИДИТ, мы ВИДИМ, вы ВИДИТЕ, они ВИДЯТ

You can notice that in the first singular person the consonant of the root of the verb integrated or modified itself. This phenomenon is called **consonant alternation** and figuring out from which infinitive a verb comes from could be annoying. Luckily, this problem is solved by the dictionary which contains the alternations.

Here a useful list of first and second conjugation verbs that you can use to practice:

First conjugation: A + Е / Ю + suffixes

делать	diélat'	to do
покупать	pakupàt'	to buy
слушать	slùshat'	to listen

133

повторять	pavtariàt'	to repeat
работать	ràbòtat'	to work
понимать	panimàt'	to understand
играть	igràt'	to play (valid also with musical instruments)

Second conjugation: И + suffixes

готовить	gatòvit'	to cook/ to make → alternation: в / вл
положить	palajìt'	to put / to lay
	spiescìt'	to hurry
смотреть	smatriét'	to watch
	dierjàt'	to hold
звонить	svanìt'	to call

Pay attention to the false friends!

СТИРАТЬ (stiràt', 1° con) does not mean "to stir up", but "to wash"! "To iron" is ГЛАДИТЬ (glàdit', 2° con).

134

10.3. Verbs that will drive you crazy, the so-called "irregular verbs"

Unfortunately or luckily, the verbs are full of peculiarities and irregularities that could create problems even to the most motivated student. The best method is facing them keeping your head held high, taking advantage of your brilliance and creativity.

We can divide the irregular verbs in groups, so that we can easily deal with them:

1. Group in in -ова- / -ева-
Take a look at the infinitive of these verbs: танцевать (tanzevàt', to dance), целовать (zelavàt', to kiss). If we make reference to the rule, we would locate them in the first conjugation group (they end in **-ать**). These verbs though, are different: during the whole conjugation the -ова- / -ева- is replaced by -у- before the suffixes.

я ТАНЦ**У**Ю   я ЦЕЛ**У**Ю
ты ТАНЦ**У**ЕШЬ   ты ЦЕЛ**У**ЕШЬ
он ТАНЦ**У**ЕТ   он ЦЕЛ**У**ЕТ

It is easy to distinguish these verbs, since they often are "modern" words deriving from foreign languages: can you guess what фотографи<u>ова</u>ть, fatagrafìravat', and комменти<u>ова</u>ть, kammientìravat' mean?

2. Group of monosyllables
There are other peculiarities when it comes to the monosyllabic verbs. Some of them are common verbs and that is

why it is important to remember the conjugation. The conjugation is really similar for some of them, creating a sort of similiarity with the suffixes of the first conjugation:

МЫТЬ: myt', to wash
мою, моешь, моет, моем, моете, моют (the O is always stressed)

ПЕТЬ: piét', to sing
пою, поёшь, поёт, поём, поёте, поют (ю or ё are always stressed)

ПИТЬ: pit', to drink
пью, пьёшь, пьёт, пьём. пьёте, пьют

ЖДАТЬ: jdat', to wait
жду, ждёшь, ждёт, ждём, ждёте, ждут

БРАТЬ: brat' , to take
беру, берёшь, берёт, берём, берёте, берут

The situation is different with the verb "to eat", since it is completely irregular:

ЕСТЬ: iést', to eat
ем, ешь, ест, едим, едите, едят
(the initial "e" is always stressed)

3. Group affected by the consonant alternation
We have already hinted at this "anomaly" that causes changes in the first singular person of some second conjugation verbs (see paragraph 10.2). This is also a problem of some first conjugation verbs that, on the contrary, change for each person.

136

Let's see some of them and then a recapitulatory scheme of the main consonant alternations.

СКАЗАТЬ: skasàt', to say
скажу, скажешь, скажет, скажем, скажете, скажут

ПИСАТЬ: pisàt', to write
пишу, пишешь, пишет, пишем, пишете, пишут

ПЛАКАТЬ: plàkat', to cry
плачу, плачешь, плачет, плачем, плачете, плачут

ИСКАТЬ: iskàt', to look for
ищу, ищешь, ищет, ищем, ищете, ищут

ДВИГАТЬ: dvìgat', to move / to shift
движу, движешь, движет, движем, движете, движут

(*Be careful to the accent: with the exception of the first person (pishù), the stress falls on the и for the other persons. Otherwise the verb has a pretty different meaning: "*to pee*"!)

Here what happens to verbs when there is the consonant alternation:

Tab. 9: CONSONANT ALTERNATION IN VERBS

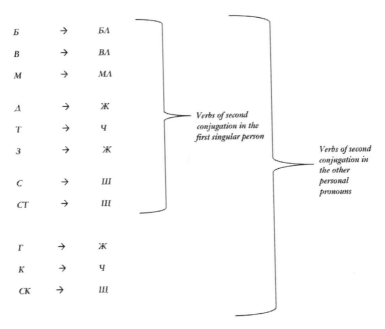

There are also other groups of peculiar Russian verbs: in a few lessons we will focus on the verbs of motion, a real closed group with specific rules.

The best way to learn verbs is using them: challenge yourself with these exercises! As always, the answers are at the end of the chapter.

EXERCISE 10

Conjugate the first conjugations verbs in brackets

1. Он _____ (рассказывать) о своей поездке в Германию.
2. Ты _____ (работать) в школе.
3. Мы _____ (читать) по-русски.
4. Вы меня хорошо _____ (понимать)?
5. Я _____ (заканчивать) сочинение.

EXERCISE 11

Choose the correct form of the second conjugation verbs

1. Ты хорошо говорите / говоришь / говорешь по-русски?
2. Мама не гладает / гладет / гладить мою одежду (my clothes).
3. Сегодня мы спешим / спешам / спешат.
4. Я готову / готовлю / готаю для друзей (for my friends).
5. Они звонут / звоняют / звонят мне.

EXERCISE 12

Complete adding the missing letters. You can help yourself with the translation.

1. Я м…ю посуду.
I wash the dishes

2. Вася фотографир… красивый город.
Vasja fotografa una bella città

3. Вы пла…те, потому что вы грустные.
You cry because you are sad

4. Аня пи…т хорошее письмо.
Anya writes a wonderful letter

5. Мы ж…м нашего друга.
We wait for our friend.

Let's disclose the secrets of this chapter

. Russian verbs are divided into two regular conjugations and also into different irregular groups.

. In order to recognize a verb in the infinitive form, you must observe the last two letters: the Russian infinitive always ends with ТЬ.

. It is possible to determine the conjugation by observing the vowel before "ТЬ": in general -АТЬ е -ЯТЬ are first conjugation verbs, ИТЬ е -ЕТЬ are the second one. Although, this is not an absolute rule.

. First and second conjugation are similar: the difference is that, in the first one, the vowel of the verb does not change and another vowel is added during the whole conjugation; in the second one the vowel stays the same and it only changes for the personal pronouns "I" and "they".

. If you want to easily memorize the irregular verbs, it is useful dividing them in similar groups.

. It is important for you to know the phenomenon of the consonant alternation: in the second conjugation there are changes just in the first singular person; in the first conjugation every person of the verb changes.

ANSWERS.

Exercise 10
1. рассказывает – He talks about his trip in Germany.
2. работаешь – You work at school.
3. читаем – We read in Russian.
4. понимаете – Do you understand me?
5. заканчиваю – I finish the text.

Exercise 11
1. говоришь – Do you speak well Russian?
2. гладит – Mom does not iron my clothes.
3. спешим – We are in hurry today.
4. готовлю – I cook for my friends.
5. звонят – They phone (call) me.

Exercise 12
1. МОЮ
2. ФОТОГРАФИРУЕТ
3. ПЛАЧЕТЕ
4. ПИШЕТ
5. ЖДЁМ

DAY 11: GRAB YOUR AGENDA

Dear reader, today I am going to cut you some slack from grammar and I want to focus on a special theme to Russians and somehow a theme that is different from our classical conception: time.

Although the universal conventions that divide the year in 12 months,the months in days and the days in 24 h each, every culture has a particular connection with time and you have to learn, know and respect it if you really want to establish a relationship with someone different from us.

Moreover, we also have to be aware of our conception of time and of the incomprehensions that could occur when we run into a different reality in which the passing of time could be perceived in a different way.

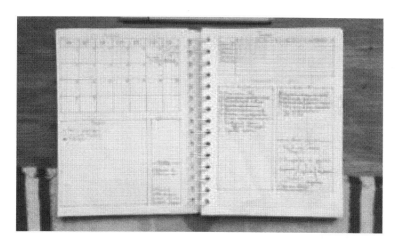

11.1. The concept of time

The Russian conception of time is composed of a mix of different influences and that is why often it is difficult to understand it. If on one hand in the big cities the concept "h24"(shops and services open 24/7) is common, on the other hand Russians do not tackle their daily activities in a chaotic way. They tolerate people being late, long times to decide something and the necessity to meditate on things; on the other hand, you can happen to see in the middle of Russian winter, women speeding on frozen streets wearing vertiginous high heels (how the hell is that possible?!), and in the rush hours in the subway people moving in quick and confident stack towards their destination.

In Russia everything is legitimate: sipping a coffee the whole evening or madly running down the arduous escalator of the subway (it is fascinating to see as much as extreme to do: it is better to stay on the right!).

You have to live in first person this strange idea of time in order to understand its infinite aspects, and it will always surprise a foreigner visiting this great country. On one hand Russia could seem a huge, slow and reflective pachyderm, but on the other hand it could be a lively and fast ferret.

You have always have to pay attention to the presence of these "two speeds" of the Russian nature.

We can partially find ourselves in these two behaviors: for example the speed with which we face our life in general, from our career and job to the free time   spent with our family and friends.

I recommend this great movie to better understand this particular Russian concept of time: "Russian Ark" " (Russkij Kovcheg), a 2002 movie by the Russian filmmaker Aleksandr Sokurov. The main characteristic of this movie is that it is just one long, continuous take (one single take, without editing). The story is set in the inside or in the adjacent area of the Hermitage Palace in Saint-Petersburg, and it is focused on fragmentary and often dreamlike situations passing through the different ages of the Russian nobility. The movie transmits at the same time a feeling of heaviness but also of lightness, and there is a quote in it that, in my opinion, perfectly explains the Russian concept of time:

"Everyone knows the future, but no one knows the past...We are destined to navigate eternally, to live eternally".

11.2. Let's stick a label on time

The best way to learn the days of the week and the months is noting them down on your agenda: you just have to repeat them for two weeks and if you are used to take a look at them everyday, you will definitely fix them in your mind!
Let's see how they work and what these names mean:

НЕДЕЛЯ = week, niediélia – ДЕНЬ = day, diégn

1. понедельник = paniediél'nik
pa+niediél'nik, meaning "at the beginning of the week": Monday

2. вторник = vtòrnik
deriving from "vtaròi", "second": "the second day of the week" is Tuesday

3. среда = sriéda
deriving from "sriédnii", "middle": "in the middle of the week", Wednesday

4. четверг = cetviérg
deriving from "cetyrie", "four": "the fourth day of the week" is Thursday

5. пятница = piàtniza
deriving from "piàt'", "five": "the fifth day of the week" is Friday

6. суббота = subbòta
deriving from the Hebrew "shabbat": Saturday

7. воскресенье = vaskrisiénie
it means "resurrection": Sunday

I have always thought that, beneath the names of the days of the week, there is a lot of the culture that we have studied: here there are different influences, but generally the system is based on the count (the second day, the middle, the fourth, etc.).

If you want to stress in which day you do something, you just have to use the construction B + accusative: this construction is useful when it comes to use it with the days of the week, since the major part of nouns are masculine or neuter, and being inanimated, the accusative form is the same as the nominative (remember? We have studied it in chapter 6!).

В понедельник, **во** вторник, в четверг, в воскресенье.
(With "Tuesday", the preposition B becomes BO for phonetic reasons: you could not be able to pronunciate it then!
With the remaining feminine days, we have to change the ending for the accusative changing in в среду, в пятницу, в субботу.

The names of the months are similar to ours and they are not so difficult:

МЕСЯЦЫ = months, miésyazzy
1. Январь	ianvàr'
2. Февраль	fievràl'
3. Март	mart
4. Апрель	apriél'
5. Май	mai
6. Июнь	iiùgn
7. Июль	iiùgl
8. Август	àvgust
9. Сентябрь	sientiàbr'
10. Октябрь	aktiàbr'

11. Ноябрь	naiàbr'
12. Декабрь	dikàbr'

If you want to say that something happens in a month, you have to use an expression similar to those of the days, but pay attention to the case! This time the construction is: В + prepositional
The gender of the months is masculine, even if a lot of them end with the soft sign. To form the prepositional you just have to add an –e at the end (removing the soft sign where it is present):
в январе, в феврале, в марте, etc.

Lastly, the year. We won't focus on numbers right now, but I will give you some useful expressions: The structure to express in which year something happens is always В + prepositional.

ГОД = year, god → irregular prepositional: году
в этом году = this year (v etom gadù)
в прошлом году = last year (v pròshlam gadù)
в будущем году = next year (v bùdushem gadù)

We can divide the year into four seasons using these expressions (this time without any preposition, just using the simple instrumental):

ВРЕМЕНА ГОДА = seasons

зимой	simòi	winter
весной	viesnòi	spring
летом	liétam	summer
осенью	òsiegniu	fall

All these expressions are the answer to the generic question Когда? (kagdà, when) or more precisely to the questions В каком месяце? (v kakòm miéciaze, in which month) or B какой день? (v kakòi diégn, in which day).

Complete these sentences as you like with the expressions of the months and the days of the week: pay attention to the two different constructions B + accusative for the days and B + prepositional for the months.

Я отдыхаю на море в _____.
(I go on holiday to the sea in the month of...)

Мы ужинаем вместе в _____.
(We have dinner together on...)

Ты не работаешь в _____.
(You do not work on...)

Вы будете в России в _____.
(You are going to be in Russia during the month of...)

EXERCISE 13

Now answer these questions: some possible solutions are at the end of the chapter.

1. В каком месяце Рождество? In which month is Christmas?
2. В каком месяце Пасха? In which month is Easter?
3. В каком месяце Масленица? In which month is Mardi Gras?
4. в каком месяце американская независимость? In which month is the American Indipendence?
5. В каком месяце Новый Год? In which month is New Year's Eve?
6. В какой день недели британцы не работают? In which day of the week the British people do not work?
7. В какой день недели начинают выходые? In which day of the week does the weekend start?
8. Когда люди отдыхают на море? When do people go on holiday at the sea?
9. Когда идёт снег? When does the snow fall?
10. Когда расцветают деревья? When do the trees bloom?

Let's disclose the secrets of this chapter

. The Russian concept of time has "two speeds": the same person can alternate quick movements, almost mechanical, to long moments of meditation. Being late is tolerated by Russians: toward foreigners a little less.

. To deeply understand the Russian conception of time, you have to immerse yourself completely in this culture.

. The general question to ask "when" is the interrogative pronoun КОГДА. Depending on the request, you can specify "in which month?" (в каком месяце) or "in which day" (в какой день).

. With the days of the week you have to use the construction B + accusative.

. With the months and the word год, "year", you have to use the construction B + prepositional.

. In order to express the seasons, you have to use the simple instrumental (without any preposition).

ANSWERS.

Exercise 13

1. В декабре. To Russians though, Orthodox Christmas is в январе.
2. В марте или ("or") в апреле. According to the Russian calendar, it can fall on the first days of May (в мае).
3. Masleniza is the Russian Mardi Gras. It always falls a week before the beginning of the Lenten fast: according to the Orthodox calendar it can happen в феврале или в марте.
4. в июле
5. В январе.
6. В воскресенье.
7. В пятницу.
8. Летом / В августе / В июле.
9. Зимой / В декабре, январе, феврале... in Russia it can also happen осенью.
10. Весной / в марте / в апреле.

DAY 12: FREE TIME

We have seen how Russians divide time, today we worry about something else: how do they use it up? In particular, what do they do in their free time?

"This is how I spend my holidays"

12.1. A new concept with ancients roots

The "free time" concept is a sort of a new thing to Russians. It is an idea deriving from the Western culture and it spread in Russia recently. This does not mean that Russians do not know how to spend their time: in the big cities you can find a lot of entertainment, and in the countryside the time is measured by the passing of seasons.

There are "cult" places where you can spend the Russian free time that have become so iconic that now they are a part of the foreign languages too: a classic example is the dacha (дача), the traditional Russian country house, where Russians spend their free time, above all during spring and summer, to run away from the hot cities. The *dacha* has an ancient origin: you can find it in a lot of literary works, and often, it is the starting point to talk about the countryside. It is not only a relaxing place away from the city chaos, but it is also the main source of fresh products: you can happen to see, during summer, old women with huge vases full of blueberries, mushrooms, pickled vegetables. Outside the city you can frequently see these women, and I can assure you that seeing that immense quantity of woodland products is really amazing (trust me, we are not used to the dimension of those mushrooms and blueberries!).

The summer spent in the *dacha* is the perfect occasion to relax and to save the "winter supplies" to preserve in every form and color.

Another traditional Russian place is the *banya* (баня), or "Russian bathhouse", a Russian version of the Finnish sauna: in the past, it was the only way to get washed in the countryside, on the contrary, today in the cities it is a meeting point to relax. Be careful, though: the *banya* is not the equivalent of a thermal center, it is rather a place to meet up with somebody, to make small talks and to take refuge from the cold. There are some famous bathhouses: in Moscow there is the *banya Sanduny* that was used as a set for the famous movie "Battleship Potemkin" (1925) by Sergey Ejzenshtein. You can also find the banya in a recent movie, really famous in Russia: in "Ироня судьбы", *The irony of Fate* (1975) the story begins in a Russian bathhouse where a group of friends is celebrating and drinking...

The sequence of events full of misunderstandings in a "very soviet style" are really funny!

12.2. Let's spend the time like a proper Russian

Today the great Russian cities are completely westernized: Saint-Petersburg is a city model born with this specific purpose; Moscow is a more complex city, a mosaic of different realities linked together to create many cities in one. As you can immagine, there is plenty of entertainment for citizens but also for tourists.

The fundamental question is: **ЧТО ТЫ ЛЮБИШЬ ДЕЛАТЬ В СВОБОДНОЕ ВРЕМЯ?**
(shto ty liùbish diélat' v svabòdnae vriémya?)
meaning "**What do you like (love) doing in your free time?**""

Let's see some answers:

ПИТЬ ЧАЙ, pit' chai

Forget about the English tradition of the 5 pm tea, a moment of pleasentries and cucumber sandwiches: to Russians, the tea is a perfect moment to celebrate with a lot of foods (sweet and savory food), to chat and to sip tea obviously. The tea is a precise ritual with an eastern origin. Moreover, the tea is not a particular drink just to celebrate something, Russians always drink it: after all, is there a better way to warm up? If you are thinking about something else, hold back your curiosity for the next chapter! During the traditional moment of the tea you will see the samovar, the iconic container so beloved to Russians, and also a lot of delicacies.

ГУЛЯТЬ ПО УЛИЦАМ, ПО ПАРКЕ, guliàt' pa ùlizam, pa pàrke

Russians love open spaces: during winter the city parks covered in snow are amazing, and you can find there a lot of people practicing winter sports like skating and, why not? ski

156

too. During summer or winter, Russians like taking advantage of the moment of relax outdoors. They have a great respect toward parks and they deeply take care of them. Imagine enjoying a park just for three months, though: it is normal put the sign "do not sit on the grass"!

ПОСЕЩАТЬ МУЗЕИ, pasieshàt' musiéi

We have to admit that the Russian culture is really huge and they are aware and so proud of it. In the years Russia cranked out a lot of talented people in all fields, from astronauts to writers, from athletes to musicians. Wherever you are it is impossible not finding trace of this glorious artistic and cultural past (or present). In the cities there is an infinite number of museums and the quantity of landmarks and famous places is so huge that a trip is not enough. So, everyone can be pleased. If a Russian friend suggests visiting museums, get ready to hear a real history lecture: Russians are deeply proud of their historical-artistic heritage.

In addition to famous museums and collections of western artworks, it is interesting immersing ourselves in something traditionally Russian, although it is not so popular: art is the perfect window from which observe and better understand a people. The most famous Russian museum is the Hermitage in Saint-Petersburg: according to a survey, you need to spend eight years of your life to observe all masterpieces! The museum includes a lot of collections coming from all over the world, and in the past a part was just for the Tsar's family.

The Russian cities offer all kind of museums: you can spend an evening in specific museums in Moscow or Saint-Petersburg finding out about how vodka is produced, or visiting one of the "house museums" dedicated to important figures of the Russian culture (such as the museum Mayakovskij in Moscow), or even observing closer some of the best creations by Fabergè, the popular decorated eggs that

157

made the Russian aristocracy go crazy. There are plenty of opportunities, and often they are not so expensive.

ИДТИ В ТЕАТР / НА БАЛЕТ, ittì v tieàtr, na baliét

Another traditional Russian pride is the theater, above all the ballet. Speaking of it, follow me in the reading of this text about the main theaters in Moscow:

Театральная площадь:
Многие знают, что Большой театр находится на Театральной площади. Но не все знают, что на этой площади не один, а три театра. Большой театр, Малый театр и Российский молодёжный театр. Большой - это театр оперы и балета, а вот Малый и Российский молодёжный - драматургические.
Приходите в Большой театр, и вы увидите замечательные спектакли, о которых знает весь мир.

translation:
Teatral'naya ploshad' (literally theater square)
A lot of people know that the Bolshoi Theater is on Teatral'naya Square. But a few people know that on this square there is not just one theater, but three theaters (не один, а три театра). Bolshoi Theater, Malyi Theater (lit. "small") and the Russian Academic Youth Theater. The Bolshoi is an Opera and ballet house, and the Malyi and the Russian Academic Youth Theater are for dramas. Come to the Bolshoi Theater and you will see wonderful plays, famous all over the world.

ЧИТАТЬ, citàt'

We have studied this verb talking about grammatical conjugations. Today we will use it to talk more about how Russians spend their free time: reading is a hobby that seems to resist to the new technologies. A simple experiment is enough to understand it: if you happen to travel by underground in Moscow or Saint-Petersburg, you will probably see a lot of people reading, no matter you are a man, a woman, young or old, that is surprising. Even if the literary Russian culture is huge, you can guess that is not so likely seeing Russians as evaluator enthusiastics of the classics: the most sold out books are detective stories (детективы, dietiektivy) and romance novels (любовные романы, liubòvnye romany).

ЗАНИМАТЬСЯ СПОРТОМ, sanimàzza spòrtam

Today the sport is really important in Russia and here a list of the main sports, both traditional and not. You will see that you won't need the translation for some of them!

футбол
воллейбол
баскетбол
теннис
плавание (даплавать, to swim)
катание = skating / фигурное катание = figure skating
ходить на лыжах = to ski
бег (from бегать, to run)

You can use different expressions when you talk about sports:
я занимаюсь* + instrumental = I play (practice)... yà sanimàius'
я играю в + <u>accusative</u>= I play... (not for all sports) – yà igràiu v...
я люблю + accusative = I love... - yà liubliù

For example: я занимаюсь бегом, я играю в воллейбол, а я люблю фигурное катание!
And if you are an hopeless lazy bones? **Я совсем не** занимаюсь спортом!

*Attention: заниматься is a reflexive verb! See chapter 10 to review how to build them.

Let's disclose the secrets of this chapter

. Russians knew how to spend their free time even before that this expression was born.

. The Russian country house, dacha and the Russian bathhouse, banya, are two of the traditional places to understand the Russian tradition of relax away from work and obligations.

. If you want to ask someone what he/she does in his/her free time, this is the question: ЧТО ТЫ ЛЮБИШЬ ДЕЛАТЬ В СВОБОДНОЕ ВРЕМЯ? (shto ty liùbish diélat' v svabòdnae vriémya?)

. The past Russian traditions weave together with the uses of the present: the ritual of the tea is a perfect example.

. Russians love culture: museums, theaters and galleries cannot wait to be visited!

. The importance of sports is growing, above all among young people: you can use different constructions to talk about the sport that you play, using the cases that we have studied in chapter 6.

DAY 13: DINNER PARTY

Dear reader, here we are at my favourite chapter, what I have been dreaming since the beginning: well, finally we talk about food! In my opinion, I think that the cuisine of a people is a necessary step to deeply understand its culture. So, today we are going to talk about the best delicacies! If a Russian friend invite you to dinner you cannot say no. They might get offended! So, it is better to be preapared for a Russian dinner.

How can you stay so unmoved in front of so much food?

13.1. The variety of the Russian cuisine

Let's start by saying that the Russian cuisine is pretty various and different from ours. We have to keep in mind that Russia is the most extended country in the world and on its territory we can find an incredible variety of people and traditions. In this chapter we will focus on the Russian traditional cuisine, with a brief introduction on the Caucasian tradition (I chose it for personal reasons, I know you will thank me!) There are some specialties that cannot be missing in a menu of a Russian restaurant, although there are a lot of variations due to the season or to the geographical area. Let's see together the main ones:

Закуски, zakùski, *starters* (literally "snacks"):
A fundamental part of every meal is reserved to those small dishes served before the main courses. If you are a guest in a Russian house for dinner, you have to know that this part of the lunch or dinner is also a moment to entertain guests. The code word of закуски is "variety": we can find different types of cheese, cold cuts, dishes made with fish (herring, trout and salmon and a lot of other fishes, whose names are difficult to be translated, I have always been unprepared in front of the fish stand in supermarkets!) or vegetables and woodland products (mushrooms in particular). This kind of culinary tradition is similar to ours, for the quantity and also for the lightness.

For obvious climatic reasons, the Russian cuisine is really fat and it makes use of a lot of products derived from milk: the butter is omnipresent (also in deep-fried dishes); another dish that cannot be missed in the side dishes is the сметана, *smietàna*, the sour cream. The Eastern European cuisines use a lot of smetana to garnish both sweet and savory dishes. At a first taste you might not like it, but you will get used to it

164

(or learn how to say not to put it in your dish, as we will learn shortly).

Супы, sùpy, *soups*:
Whatever the season, hot or cold, soups (or broth) cannot be missing in a Russian lunch or dinner. Among the most famous ones we can find борщ, borsch, a soup made with beetroots, marked out by its intense and bright pink color, almost violet. From a chromatic point of view it is not so tempting, but it is interesting its cold version in summer; щи, schi, a simple soup made with cabbage; солянка, salyànka, in different versions (with meat, fish or mushrooms), with its typical spiced taste, usually served hot.

Первые и вторые блюда, piérvye i vtaryìe bliùda, *first and second courses*:
There is a great variety of first and second dishes too. There is not a neat separation beteween "first" and "second" courses: you'd rather find these categories divided in sub-groups depending on the type of dish:

- **пельмени**, piel'miéni, dumplings filled with meat, fish, cheese, potatoes, mushrooms or vegetables. They are combined with smeatana and dill (укроп, commonly known as зелень, seliégn, a word that is for all aromatic herbs), the Russian parsley. A variant with a different form (half moon) are the **вареники**, variéniki; you can also find a sweet version of them.

- **блины**, bliny, the Russian version of crepes or pancakes. They are so traditional that the term entered the western language. You can find both sweet and savory versions of them, and you can eat them with everything: from the cherry jam to the salmon, from bananas to the caviar. There are also Russian fastfoods for blinys, as the famous Теремок with its great variety of this food. Bliny are the passepartout of the Russian cuisine and everyone loves them!

- **мясо и рыба**, myàsa i ryìba, meat and fish: everytime is hard to decide. Yes, it is hard because it is not easy to decide if try the beef Stroganoff (говядина по-строгановски, sautèed pieces of beef served with sour cream) or the various recipes based on herrings, salmon etc.. Why not try both?

Десерты, diesérty, *desserts*:
A sweet taste to finish the meal: you have to consider all the sweet versions of the savory dishes we have already talked about, but I would add пироги, piròghi, little tarts. They are cooked in the oven and they are made of dough filled in various ways (and guess what? There is also a savory version!). The most distinctive characteristic of these tarts is the decoration on the surface , a sort of embroidery made with dough to reproduce writings, drawings or simply decorations typical of the Russian tradition. There are also the пирожки, literally "small savory pies", common in the savory version and served hot with different kind of filling; they are perfect for a quick snack or for a lunch outdoors.

I hope you are getting hungry because now we will see practically how to order all these delicacies at the table of a restaurant.
First, let's make a call to reserve a table:

- Алло (Hello?)
- Алло. Можно заказать стол на 3 человека, сегодня вечером? (Hello, good morning. I would like to reserve a table for three for this evening).
- Да. В котором часу? (Sure, what time?)
- В восемь часов. (8 pm).
- Хорошо. Как вас зовут? (Good. What is your name?)

166

- Коля. (Kolya.)
- Стол на 3, в восемь часов вечера на имя "Коля". (A table for three at 8 pm, name Kolya.)
- Хорошо, до встречи. (All right. See you this evening!)
- До встречи. (Goodbye!)

It does not matter if it is обед or ужин (abiéd, lunch, ùjin, dinner), you will find yourself sit at your стол (stol, table) with an официант (afizànt, waiter, or afizàntka, waitress) ready to take your order: you won't need any kind of formality and forms of courtesy, since the Russian restaurants are pretty informal places (obviously we are talking about restaurants for all budgets).

If you want to order something you just need to say "Для меня…" (dlyà minyà), meaning "for me…", and then the name of the dish that you want. The Russian menu is divided following the order that we have already seen: in a separated menu you can find the list of drinks (напитки) and also the wine list (винная карта). Do not forget the basic forms of courtesy that we have learned in the first chapters: a спасибо is always welcome, even to the most surly waiter.

Moreover, you have to know that in Russia there is a type of food service similar to our fast foods: it is called столовая, literally "cafeteria", a place where you can eat self-service depending on the courses exposed following the classic Russian menu (закуски, супы, …).
They are a good choice particularly for the lunch, since it is not necessary to wait for the service and they are also pretty cheap. You just have to choose beforehand what to eat: Russians do not tolerate indecision when it comes to wait in line.

If the Russian cuisine does not trigger the spark of unconditional love in you, don't worry! You definitely will find the way to satiate your appetite thanks to the great variety of restaurants and cuisines from all over the world, above all in the great Russian cities (they are spreading, though: from суши, often "revisited" with Russian ingredients, to the Caucasian tradition, until any kind of typical cuisine of all great cities).

In my opinion, you absolutely have to try the Georgian cuisine that offers culinary options between the Russian tradition, the Middle Eastern one and the mountain one: among the dishes you can find flat bread with goat cheese, dumplings filled with meat or mushrooms (in their traditional "chef's hat" shape), different types of meat cooked on the grill and simply called "kebap", and in the end different choices of desserts. Besides, recently the trade sanction on the importation of Georgian wine to Russia concluded, so today it is possible to quaff it during an already perfect dinner, adding some more perfection.

So, once you have chosen carefully a good restaurant, following the advices of a friend or of a local, you surely won't be unsatisfied, because there really is something for everyone. Russians love eating and they do it at any time. For this reason, they still have difficulties to accept some food "particularisms" that are quickly spreading in the West: it is rare finding vegetarian and even rarer vegan restaurants. Often, people with food intolerances or with health problems are disadvantaged: if you belong to these categories, here a few useful sentences like

я не могу есть … (I cannot eat)
у меня аллергия на … (I am allergic to)
без + genitive (without)

It is important that you specify to the waiter that you have a health problem and not just a request of yours (like the movie "When Harry met Sally…"!).

If, on the contrary, you cannot stop eating, hurry up and find a Russian restaurant in your city!

13.2. The half empty glass

Russians are great drinker, that is a clichè: although this is not the absolute truth for everyone, we have to admit that in Russia drinking alcoholic beverages is a rooted tradition. First of all, climatic conditions are fundamental: how can you survive at a temperature of -30° remaining perfectly tee-total? Unfortunately, alcoholism is a serious society problem, but at the same time it is an important part of the meal and above all of the celebrations!

The word vodka, водка, comes from вода (vadà, water), and it literally means "little water": it is not a light drink at all, it can cause a powerful migraine and also stomach burning and other ailments. Unless you well take alcohol (and believe me Russia could change your mind!), I recommend not to launch yourself in a drinking competition with Russian friends; moreover, if you are having dinner with Russians, they surely will fill your glass everytime it is empty, as a form of courtesy and hospitality. Make sure to leave a drop of vodka in your glass if you are not ready to follow the Russian drinking pace!

Don't worry: there are alternatives to vodka and you absolutely have to try them once: besides the common drinks that we have in Europe (a great selection of beers – **pivo** – with different tastes and alcoholic degrees), Russians have a particular tradition of beverages that could not satisfy you at a first taste. Here some of the most particular ones that I have tasted during my trips:

- Квас, **kvas**, a fermented beverage produced with different products: fruit or berries, cereals or birch juice even. The final result is an intense fermented flavour, similar to the dark beer. When you try the kvas is like you are drinking and eating at the same time! During the Soviet period the kvas was considered a refreshing beverage (they still think it is!)

- Тархун, **tarkhùn**, a beverage of Georgian origin made with tarragon and other aromatic herbs. It is a bright green drink and its taste is something between the sweet and the pungent of mint. In the parks, during summer, you can find stands where you can buy fresh lemonade and other drinks: among them you can also find the tarkhùn. It can be refreshing but with a strange sweetish note, not always convincing.

- Кисель, **kisiél'** is something between a drink and a jelly, it is made with fruit (mainly berries) and it is served like a dessert. As the other two beverages, the kisiél' can be homemade by following the traditional recipe but also by using a mix available in supermarkets. I have tasted it as a drink during a snack break together with the bliny and also as a dressing for the bliny. A really versatile product!

Let's disclose the secrets of this chapter

. Russian cuisine is varied and nutritious. You can find a lot of dishes both in hot or cold version.

. The main products of Russian courses are the smetana (sour cream) and dill, as well as basic ingredients like cabbage and potatoes.

. In the big Russian cities there are a lot of international restaurants: the Russian version of sushi (суши) and the Caucasian cuisine, in particular the Georgian cuisine are interesting options.

. Vodka is not an easy subject, in particular with the empty stomach.

. Russians are great drinkers: do not try imitating them!

. There are also alternatives to vodka and you have to try them: квас, тархун е кисель are just some of the various flavors waiting for you!

DAY 14: RUSSIA IS BIG

So far we have talked about Russia as a whole, but we cannot ignore this aspect: Russia is big, bigger than any other country in the world!

You can notice it even in the little things: in my case it was almost immediate, exactly when I got the Saint-Petersburg airport. The Russian guy that had to pick my classmates and me up, had perfectly eastern traits, but he had not any kind of Russian inflexion when he spoke.

These apparent contradictions can be explained looking at a map. And the same map can be explained studying the history of this huge country.

14.1. A brief history lesson

The Russian history is complex and fascinating and it cannot be summarized in a few lines. Nevertheless, a foreigner that visits Russia has to know, generally speaking, the most important events and the different historical evolutions, in order to understand the reasons of the main daily aspects. Moreover, it is important knowing history so you can be in line with the people that you will meet, because history inevitably is part of our life – and in Russia this is pretty clear.

The Russian history can be divided into four periods:
1. the general period dating from the foundation of the reign of Kiev to the Tsar Peter the Great (9th cenury- 1700);

2. the Tsarist imperial Russia (1721-1917);

3. the Soviet Union (from the October revolution in 1917 to 1989-1990);

4. the Russian Federation (from the 90's to current year).

The important thing to remember is that the historical Russian developments were complex and the passage from a period to another has always been full of conflicts and sufferings. The rifts inside the society have always been the key to understand Russian history: still today, in the modern Russia, there is a great social gap between rich and poor that determines a major part of the daily life (in Moscow high fashion boutiques and suburban and poor neighborhoods coexist, whereas in the countryside the lifestyle remained the same as years and years ago).
Russians talk about their past with great respect and melancholy: it is better avoiding direct questions (even if for us, born and raised in the opposite part of the Iron Curtain,

wondering how they lived in those years is spontaneous); the right thing to do when it comes to take on a conversation about historical themes, is carefully paying attention without urging who is talking.

Still today, in the largest cities, there are visible proofs of the various historical periods, often mixed up: the most common example is the Red Square in Moscow (Красная Площадь, because the root крас- in ancient Russian used to mean *beautiful* – today красивый). In the immense space of 74.831 sq.m. the historical proofs of different periods coexist and they are something like a "summary" of Russia in the whole: the Kremlin walls (from Russian кремль, *fortress*), that enclose the center of the Russian authority, as well as bear witness of the pre and post Tsarist period; the cathedral of Vasily the Blessed (yes, people wrongly call it "the Kremlin"), built by Tsar Ivan the Terrible in 1561 to celebrate the victory on the Tatars; the State Historical Museum, a building dating back to the first half of the 19th century, containing a lot of historical finds dating even back to the Paleolithic (this is a lot of history!); the Lenin's Mausoleum, as the resting place of Lenin in person (conserved with a technique of taxidermy that still is state secret), surrounded by the graves of other Soviet personalities; the State Department Store GUM (Главный Универсальный Магазин), built at the end of the 19th century and considered as a symbol of consumerism, spread in Russia with the fall of the Soviet regime.

You will be asking yourself how many historical events can coexist in the same place: the truth is that Russia is still affected by its past and sufferings that were typical of the passage from a period to the other.

It is impossible not to notice the traces of the Russian history in every corner of the city, but you have to have a good sight and a lot of curiosity.

14.2. A brief geography lesson

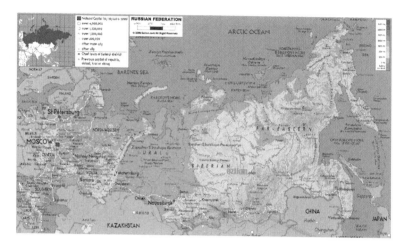

How really big is Russia? And how is it possible that a huge country like Russia is just one State with a single language and a single culture?

The answer to the first question is the simplest one: the Russian territory is 17.098.242 kmq, the first country in the world for extension. For the second question

I have to give you some more information: first of all, although it is huge, Russia is not likewise populated! Think about the fact that in certain areas just one inhabitant for kmq is counted. This fact is not surprising if you consider the climate matter.

So, it is an extended country but not so populated. This population is composed of various ethnic groups, each with its own traditions and also language and religion (the second religion for numbers of worshippers is Islamism, and in specific areas of Siberia shaman rituals still exist).

The advantage (or disadvantage in terms of cultural plurality) brought by the Soviet Union was making the population literate: for this reason, the Russian language is a useful tool in every zone of the country, even if in certain cases it undergoes the influence of other languages spoken in the near territories (above all at the boundary with China and central Asia).

EXERCISE 14

The trip that every Russia lover wish to carry out once in life is the trans-Siberian railway, the famous railway that crosses the whole Russian territory from Moscow to Vladivostok. Imagine you are on a train and you have to explain to your friend your stop-overs. Follow the example.

ex. Я еду от Москвы до Нижнего Новгорода = I go from Moscow to Nijnyi Novgorod

от + genitive до + genitive = from...to...

Я еду от Нижнего Новгорода до ...(Новосибирск)
Я еду от ... до ... (Новосибирск - Красноярск)
Я еду от ... до ... (Красноярск - Иркутск)
Я еду от ... до ... (Иркутск - Чита)
Я еду от ... до ... (Чита - Хабаровск)
Я еду от ... до Владивостока. (Хабаровск)
The stop-overs on the map are the following:
Novosibirsk, Krasnojarsk, Irkutsk, Chita, Khabarovsk, Vladivostok (Новосибирск, Красноярск, Иркутск, Чита, Хабаровск, Владивосток).

This is not the only trans-Siberian way possible, there are other routes for travellers depending on their necessities, on the length of the trip and also on the period of the year.

14.3. Moscow or Saint-Petersburg?

Here we are, dear reader, in front of the dilemma that sooner or later assails every Russia lover: is it better Moscow or Saint-Petersburg?

Let's start by saying that the decision is subjective: both cities were capitals in different periods (Sain-Petersburg was built by Tsar Peter the Great and it is an actual *ad hoc* imperial city; Moscow became again capital with the Soviet Union and it still is today in the modern era); both proudly show the scars and the splendour of the past, and both are populated by people that are deeply proud to live there.

Often in the debate it is said, to the advantage of Moscow, that it is the "true Russian city" in disadvantage of Saint-Petersburg, defined an "Italian city" since the origin of the architects that built and decorated it between 18th and 19th century. Some people are "pro Saint-Petersburg" and they prefer it because it is more orderly, modern, "western", a vision that was present even in the past (as a matter of fact that is exactly what Peter the Great wanted when he built it).

This discussion has been going on for centuries not only among the foreigners who love Russia, but also among Russians! Often a lot of them claim that the Moscow citizens are more "coarse" in comparison with the Saint-Petersburg ones, considered more elegant and kind, as heir of some lost nobility.

Well, this is my suggestion: take an airplane as soon as possible and visit both so that you will get a better idea in first person!
They are both beautiful cities and they will become even better once you will have your personal memories.

What are you waiting for? It is time to leave: Russia is big and it takes time to visit it properly!

Let's disclose the secrets of this chapter

. Russian history helps to better understand a lot of aspects of the present.

. Russian history can be divided into four large periods: from the foundation to the Empire, from the Empire to 1917, the Soviet Union and the modern Russian Federation.

. Every historical period is visible in different areas of the great cities: the Red Square in Moscow is a clear example.

. For its geography, Russia is the largest country in the world.

. On the Russian territory, different ethnic groups and cultures coexist together. The Russian language can be a useful tool for the whole territory.

. The dilemma Moscow vs. Saint Petersburg affects everybody, Russians included. It is better if you get an idea in first person visiting them as soon as possible!

ANSWERS.

Exercise 14

Я еду от Нижнего Новгорода до Новосибирск
Я еду от Новосибирска до Красноярска.
Я еду от Красноярска до Иркутска.
Я еду от Иркутска до Читы.
Я еду от Читы до Хабаровска.
Я еду от Хабаровска до Владивостока.

DAY 15: WHO ARE UNCLE AND AUNT?

Russians are deeply bound to the concept of family, a real nest where the children can feel cuddled and also a little spoiled, and the older ones respected and listened. The Russian literature is scattered of stories of great families where the tangles and relations are really complicated.

Nowadays Russian families are not different from ours: they love spending time in family and share this joy with others. If you want to talk about your family you will need the words in the following paragraph.

15.1. "All happy families look alike"

From the famous incipit of "Anna Karenina", Tolstoj makes us understand that there is no difference between families as long as they are happy: the Russian sentence is Все счастливые семьи похожи друг на друга (vsié shastlìvye siemì pakhòji drug na drùga), in which the most important word is СЕМЬЯ, simyà, family.

Be careful: in Russian the word фамилия means "last name" (it is the classic "false friend" and we are going to focus on it in the next paragraph).
Who is part of the Russian семья? We have already used the majority of these words:

feminine:
мама = mom
сестра = sister
бабушка = grandma
дочка = daughter
девочка = little girl
жена = wife
тётя = aunt

masculine:
папа* = dad
брат = brother
дедушка* = grandpa
сын = son
мальчик = little boy
муж = husband
дядя* = uncle

*Remember? Even if "papa", "diédushka" and "dyàdia" end with А/Я, they are logically considered masculine nouns! For the plural you have to pay particular attention: if you are talking about "children" in general, you have to use the term дети, diéti, *children* (it can be used only in plural; in singular form you have to use the masculine and femenine equivalents of мальчик and девочка or the unisex version – grammatically masculine - **ребёнок**). A person can refer to his /her own children by using дети even if they are adults since quite a while!

On the contrary, the word to point out the *parents* is родители, radìtieli, one of the many words deriving from the root **род**- that stresses both the concepts of being born and generating.

But you will be asking yourself why I chose a mysterious title for this chapter about family: yes, who are uncle and aunt? You have to know that in Russian the words дядя and тётя (uncle and aunt) are also used in a colloquial way to refer to people that do not belong to the family, used in particular by children. It is not a rare thing hearing these words attributed to perfect strangers:

ex. "Мам, куда этот дядя идёт?"= mom, where is that guy going?

In addition, remember that the words concerning the family are the most puzzling: irregularities, masculine names that could seem feminine and a lot of diminutive versions and hypocorisms.

Take a look at the sentence of the example: мам is clearly an abbreviated form of мама, but since the mom is always the mom, we can find other nice names such as

мамочка

матушка

маменька
мамуля
мамка

...

So, a Russian kid knows how to convince his / her mom to obtain what he / she wants. Clearly, these infinite forms of diminutive-hypocorisms are possible for all the nouns concerning the family: after all, a lot of them are a real invention and for this reason it is always possible to create new versions.

EXERCISE 15

Read the text about Ivan's family, translate it and answer the questions (the answers at the end of the chapter)

У Ивана есть большая семья. У него есть мама, Ирина, и папа, Сергей. У родителей (*plur.gen. of родители*) Ивана есть ещё дочка, Люся. Люся – младшая (younger) сестра Ивана. Папа Сергей – единственный сын, а у мамы есть сестра и брат, Наташа и Юрий. Мужа Наташи зовут Карло, он испанец. Юрий не женат, но у него есть невеста (girlfriend), Катя. У Ивана есть тоже бабушка и дедушка: они – родители его папы, их зовут Мария и Павел. Может быть в будущем году у Ивана будет (future: *Ivan will have*) также кузен или кузина, потому что тётя Наташа сейчас беременна (she is pregnant).

Answer the questions: true (правильно - П) or false (неправильно - Н)?

1. Маму Ивана зовут Мария.   П / Н
2. Папа Ивана – единственный сын.   П / Н
3. Иван – младший брат Люси.   П / Н
4. У тёти Наташи есть муж.   П / Н
5. Бабушка и дедушка Ивана – родители его мамы. П / Н
6. Мама Ивана сейчас беременна.   П / Н

15.2. Russian names

What really surprises a foreigner who wants to get closer to the Russian culture is that reading, watching movies or listening to tales he/she cannot help noticing the huge variety of Russian names. More precisely, the variety of their possible versions. For example, the name Ivan (remember that the correct Russian pronunciation is Ivàn!): Ivan can develop different personalities depending on the situations of his life

Ваня
Ванюшка
Ванечка
Ванька
Ванюша
...and so on and so forth!

Often the nicknames of masculine Russian names end with **a** (or **я**), because the diminutives are formed by adding -шка -ша -чка -ка at the end of the words, both masculine or feminine.

Let's see the main Russian names and their equivalent nickname: pay attention to the pronunciation!

masculine first names:
Александр → Саша
Алексей → Алёша
Антон → Антоша
Борис → Боря (**Barìs**)
Василий → Вася
Владимир → Вова (**Vladìmir**)
Дмитрий → Дима
Игорь → Горя (**Ìgar**)
Михаил → Миша

Николай → Коля
Павел → Паша
Пётр → Петя
Сергей → Серёжа
Фёдор → Федя
Юрий → Юра

feminine first names:
Александра → Саша (identical to masculine!)
Анастасия → Настя (**Anastasìa**)
Анна → Аня
Дария → Даша
Екатерина → Катя
Елена → Лена (**Ieliéna**)
Ирина→ Ира
Любовь → Люба (as common noun, lyubòv' means «love»
and it is feminine)
Мария → Маша
Надежда → Надя (nadezhda means «hope»)
Наталия → Наташа
Ольга → Оля
Светлана → Света
София → Соня (**Safìa**)
Татьяна → Таня

These are just some of the infinite nicknames that can be
created. Russians love using hypocorisms or diminutives
above all between friends and in family.
In other contexts though, they use a different name: the extended Russian name is made of three parts, NAME +
PATRONYMIC + LAST NAME
The patronymic is new to us: it is made from the name of
the father adding then **ович/евич** for masculine names,
овна/евна for feminine ones.

191

ex. Борис Николаевич = Boris, Nikolaj's son; Наталия Юревна = Nataliya, Jurij's daughter.

The combination "name+patronymic" is common in formal situations too, such as in the work environment. On the contrary, the use "name+last name" is more rare: you'd rather happen to hear the complete form "name+patronymic+last name" just in official contexts.
A Russian could introduce himself / herself by using first name and patronymic, or just the name, abbreviated probably. In the written form, the patronymic is abberviated with the initial followed by a full stop.

Since we do not have patronymics, Russians love "creating" them on their model and so they could ask you the name of your father.

The Russian last names can have different endings, but you have to remember that you have to distinguish between masculine and feminine last name, as in the patronymic: the most common are those ending in
ов / ова, ев / ева, ёв / ёва
ин / ина
ский / ская
ой / ая

EXERCISE 16

Which were the last names of these Russian characters' wives? Make the feminine form of the last name (answers at the end of the chapter):

Лев Н. Толстой и София А. _____

Леонид И. Брежнев и Виктория П. _____

Фёдор М. Достоевский и Анна Г. _____

And what was the last name of Anna Karenina's husband?

_____

Let's disclose the secrets of this chapter

. Family is translated семья, simyà, and Russians love this concept: ther is no better time than the one spent with the beloved ones.

. Some nouns concernig male roles in family seem feminine, like папа and дядя. These are exceptions of the masculine that grammatically follow the feminine structure.

. With the names of the family it is possible to create an infinite variety of hypocorisms and diminutives.

. The names of a person can be "distorted" in a lot of nicknames and diminutives: you can get lost if you do not recognize them!

. Both masculine and feminine names can be abbreviated with A / Я at the end: be careful, do not be confused!

. The complete Russian name is composed of name – patronymic - last name, but this combination is just used in formal and official situations: between friends and in family you can use just the name, often abbreviated; in more formal contexts (like in the work environment, or to refer to a teacher in school), you can use name+patronymic.

ANSWERS.

Exercise 15
Translation:

Ivan has a large family. He has a mom, Irina, and a dad, Sergej/ Ivan's parents have a daughter too, Ljusya. Ljusja is Ivan's younger sister/ His dad Sergej is an only child, while his mom has a sister and a brother, Natasha and Yurij/ Natasha's husband is Carlos, he is spanish. Yurij is not married, but he has a girlfriend, Katya. Ivan has a grandma and a grandpa too: they are his father's parents, their names are Mariya and Pavel. Maybe the next year Ivan will be having a cousin, since his aunt Natasha is now pregnant.

1. Маму Ивана зовут **Мария**.
   → неправильно: её зовут Ирина
2. Папа Ивана – единственный сын.
   правильно
3. Иван – **младший** брат Люси.
   → неправильно: он старший* брат
4. У тёти Наташи есть муж.
   правильно
5. Бабушка и дедушка Ивана – родители его **мамы**.
   → неправильно: … его папы
6. **Мама** Ивана сейчас беременна.
   → неправильно: Тётя

*Older

Exercise 16
Толстая; Брежнева; Достоевская;

the husband of the unlucky Anna Karenina was Aleksej Karenin

195

DAY 16: FEELING COMFORTABLE AT HOME

Once overtaken the initial block of indifference that Russians seem to put toward the others, they are really welcoming people and to them it is important making you feel more than a simple guest when they invite you home.
How is a typical Russian house?

The traditional wooden houses, although being fascinating, they are far away from the city center, but you can enjoy their articulate and fairy architecture during an excursion outdoors!

16.1. How to describe the house: from *kvartíra* to *dvoriéz*

Let's take two type of families as an example and let's see how they describe their houses: the Ivanony live in a квартира and the Romanovy in a дворец.

Меня зовут Сергей Михайлович Иванов. Моя семья живёт в квартире. Квартира — маленькая, но уютная. Она находиться в центре города. У неё есть кухня, ванная и две спальни, одна для меня с женой и другая для детей. У нас нет гостиной, потому что не хватает пространства. Мы готовим и едим на кухне. Мы любим нашу квартиру.

Я – Николай Александрович Романов. Мы с семьёй живём в огромном дворце далеко от города. У нас много комнат: спальные, гостиные, длинные коридоры полны произведений исскуства. У дворца четыре этажа: я даже не знаю сколько у нас комнат и залов. Я никогда не посетил весь мой дворец.

You have surely noticed that the two families have completely opposite lifestyles: the Ivanovy live in a small and comfortable apartment in the city center (квартира, маленькая и уютная, в центре города); the Romanovy, on the contrary, live outside the city, in a four-story building with a lot of rooms, so numerous that Nikolaj could not be able to say the number (Я никогда не посетил весь мой дворец = I have never visited the whole building).

These two brief texts can give you an idea of two of the large variety of Russian lifestyles: the first one is more linked to the city, so it is a life confined into spaces and time in which the kitchen has a central role, for this reason there is no living room (гостиная); the second Russia is the noble one, the one that survived until the beginning of the 20th century with its sumptuous buildings, far away from cities, in time and in space too.

Nowadays the Russian house is more affected by the first tradition, even if the so-called "new Russians" are looking for a more impudent splendour (see chapter 24).

The most common word to refer to the house is **ДОМ**. This word follows some particular rules in terms of cases: if you want to say "I am at home" you have to use дома, dòma (я дома); if you want to specify a movement, "I go home" you have to say "я иду **домой**" (yà idù damòi). In the other cases it follows the regular declension, but it is better for you to memorize these two cases since they are really common.

If you are a guest in a Russian house, expect hospitality but do not expect exaggerated comforts: a lot of apartments in the big cities were built during the Soviet era and still today they show that kind of structure. We are going to focus on it in a few, now let's see some useful words.

Take a look at the map in the next page and try to understand the meaning of these terms:
гостиная
кухня
ванная
санузел (туалет)
спальная
коридор

You probably noticed that some of these nouns end in -ая and they are feminine adjectives. Hypothetically they are matched with the noun комната (kòmnata, room) but in the common use they became independent. They are conjugated like adjectives.

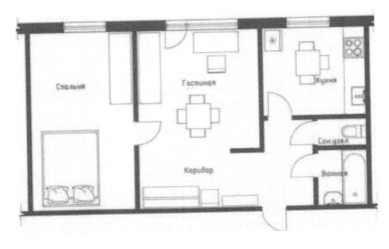

In the best case, you will find yourself in a house with defined and independent spaces. In the worst case... well, you will have to adapt yourself and sleep in the living room (гостиная), or in the kitchen (кухня), where often you can find a sofa next to the table; why not? The hallway can become habitable too, with the right arrangement. You have to notice that the bathroom is divided in two rooms, common in other European countries too: the actual ванная with the sink and the tub (used as a shower too), and the санузел (or туалет), term composed of санитарный узел, a little room where you can stay alone with the toilet and your thoughts (never forget the paper toilet!).

The interior of a typical Russian apartment is simple: wallpaper and wooden furniture, a lot of carpets (hung up on walls too) and a wooden, carpet or linoleum floor and tiles in the bathroom. Russians love to collect objects, so it is not a rare thing seeing houses full of personal souvenirs, sometimes put in a chaotic order. You will also find books, photos and theater tickets scattered everywhere.

I won't hide the fact that this could become a little suffocating for a person who is used to have a tidy house: Russians are often hoarders and to them everything can come in handy sooner or later, in a way or in the other.

So, a broken fridge turns out to be a closet, and the veranda/balcony can become a utility room, maybe "на всякий случай" (for every need).

In Russia the domestic lifestyle is characterised by a great adaptation spirit typical of a western person, first of all for what concerns the personal space. Let's see what I am talking about.

16.2. Kommunalki, krushovki: the heritage of the Soviet building industry

Russians have a different idea of the space and of the social distances. This can also be explained from a historical point of view: during the Soviet era, society was completely reshaped on the basis of a totalitarian ideology that used to consider the substantial equality of every citizen. During the first years of USSR (Union of Soviet Socialist Republics, in Russian CCCP, Союз Советских Социалистических Республики) a great part of the population moved from the countryside to the cities and for this reason a building planning was necessary.

So, the regime built the *kommunalki* (коммуналки, коммунальные квартиры), common apartments obtained by "cutting" the great aristocatic apartments: every family occupied a room or part of it, and they shared the bathrooms and the kitchen with other families.

The Soviet construction industry went through other phases, such as the хрущёвки, built in the 50's during the Nikita Khruscëv's government, named after him: they were five-story buildings, some of them still exist, built in every part of the Soviet territory following precise rules that aimed to reproduce the exact domestic scheme in every apartment. Here, the apartments had their own bathrooms, but they were so small: from 30 to 60 sq.m. depending on the number of rooms that were up to a family for its number of members.

Even now, and especially in the housing developments of the suburbs, it is so evident how this type of building is a real eyesore: with the passing of times the numbers of floors of the houses increased, but the schematic logic of construction was the same. If you want to get an idea of what it meant from the point of view of the territory, I recommend the movie "*Ирония Судьбы*", a Russian classic (I have already mentioned it in the chapter 12 and you can easily find it on the Internet): the main character, after a drink with his friends, is wrongly boarded on an airplane to Sain-Petersburg where he lands still drunk. Then he takes a taxi and he gives the driver his address, that obviously it is identical to his in Moscow. Even if he begins to recover from drunkness, our character surprisingly gets not only the wrong house, but also the wrong city! But he does not notice anything until he comes in (with his keys!) in his homonym aprtment in Saint-Petersburg. This apparently absurd comedy is based on the reality of a building industry that deeply modelled the Russian city planning of those years, and that still survives.

Let's disclose the secrets of this chapter

. The typical Russian house is the apartment, generally pretty small.

. There are different terms to refer to a house depending on the type, it can be an apartment – квартира – or an aristocratic building – дворец. Without any doubts the most generic type is дом, home.

. Remember: я – дома = I am at home; я иду домой = I go home.

. The map of a Russian house is different from ours: the bathroom is divided in two rooms and often the kitchen and the living room are a unique space.

. Russians have the habit to collect objects and so their houses look like museums of personal history.

. The standardised building industry of the Soviet era still today leaves traces in the construction of houses, in the cities, but also in the suburbs.

DAY 17: LET'S DEAL WITH THE PAST

As you know deeply a Russian, you will notice that they are really talkative people and they love talking about their own story. So, you must know how to use the verbs in the past tense. In English we have four verbal forms for the past: simple past, past continuous, past perfect and past perfect continuous too. Russians (lucky them!) love simplifying the concept of past in a unique tense, the PAST: there is just one past tense if you happen to talk about the australopithecus Lucy or about your last holidays in Indonesia.

And the incredible and super useful turning point is that you can use it also to make the conditional and the subjunctive (by adding the particle"бы"): this is a good news, isn't it?

17.1. A simple grammar (finally!)

Today I have other good news for you: you will find out that conjugating verbs in the past tense is a real godsend, in comparison with our forms of past tenses!
Explaining it by words is maybe more complicated than putting it into practice: keep in mind that when it comes to make the past tense you have always to look at the subject it is referred to, and especially gender and number of the subject (as it happens for the adjectives).
For example, let's see the conjugation in the past of the verb БЫТЬ, to be:

singular masculine	БЫЛ
singular feminine	БЫЛА
singular neuter	БЫЛО
plural form	БЫЛИ

This method to make the past tense of the verb is useful not only because it spares you the trouble of the suffixes that we have learned fort the present tense, but also because it makes you understand the identity of the subject in the moment you read a sentence in the past: in this way you can avoid any kind of misinterpretation concerning names, for example

Ваня был в Париже в прошлом году. = Vanya **has been** in Paris last year
Валя была в магазине и купила хлеба. =Valya **has been** to the grocery shop and she has bought some bread.

The masculine / feminine verb makes you understand the gender of the subject when you have doubts on first names (Vanya is male, Ivan, while Valya is female, Valentina).

Generally speaking the past tense of the verbs is made following this rule:

infinitive of the verb without **–ТЬ** +
- Л   masculine
- ЛА   feminine
- ЛО   neuter
- ЛИ   plural

The rule is the same for the reflexive verbs, but pay attention to the reflexive suffix:

заниматься = to practice / to study
занима- + Л + **ся**
занима- + ЛА / ЛО / ЛИ + **сь**

The particle **ся** is used when the verb ends with a consonant, the final **сь** (that sounds like a prolonged S) if it ends with a vowel.

Lastly, as I have mentioned at the beginning, this Russian past is also used to make complex tenses such as the subjunctive and the conditional: you just need to put the particle **бы** before or behind it:

Если бы он больше занимался, он был **бы** хорошим студентом
= If he studies, he will be a good student.

This is the typical structure of the hypothetical sentence.

For the Russian past tense the conjugation of the verb depends on the gender and number of the subject:

я   ГОТОВИЛ / ЛА / ЛО
           ГОТОВИЛ / ЛА / ЛО
он / она / оно   ГОТОВИЛ / ЛА / ЛО

masculine / feminine/ neuter singular subject

мы   ГОТОВИЛИ
вы   ГОТОВИЛИ
оин   ГОТОВИЛИ

plural subject

EXERCISE 17

Make the past of the following verbs

- писать, курить, посещать, читать, петь, мыть, сидеть
(to write, to smoke, to visit, to read, to sing, to clean, to sit)

- учиться, улыбаться, смеяться, нравиться*
(to study, to smile, to laugh, to like)

* нравиться is a verb that is used with the dative: МНЕ НРАВИТСЯ = I like

In order to define the gender of the verb in the past tense, you have to look at the grammatical subject of the sentence, not the logical one (that would be Мне):
Мне нравится яблоко = I like the apple →Мне нравилось яблоко

Мне нравится девушка = I like a girl →Мне нравилась девушка

17.2. Let's practice with the past tense

In this section I recommend two exercises to observe the interaction between the two verbal tenses (present and past) that you have studied until now:

EXERCISE 18
Read the dialogue and answer the questions. As always, the answers are at the end of the chapter.
А вы уже были в Кремле?
Мой друг живёт в Москве уже год.А я приехал недавно.
Я спросил его:
- Стив, ты можешь показать мне интересные места в Москве? Думаю, ты уже всё знаешь здесь.
- Я знаю только, где мой офис и мой дом. Понимаешь, я всё время работаю.
- Понимаю... Но я думаю, в центре ты был!
- Да,был. Вчера мы (я и наш новый клиент из Токио) были в Кремле и на Красной площади. Шеф просил показать (= il capo mi ha chiesto di portarlo li).
- Ты был вчера на Красной площади первый раз?!
- Да. И в Кремле тоже. Ты знаешь, я не ожидал, Москва - красивый город!
- А твоя жена где была в Москве?
- Она была в универмаге "Москва", в ГУМе, в ЦУМе, в ИКЕЕ, в Стокманне, в Бенеттоне, в бутике "Пьер Карден". Да, она видела многое в Москве. Это я понял, когда увидел свой счёт (=bank statement) в банке.

Questions:
1.Где живёт Стив? (Where does Steve live?)
Где он уже был? (Where has he already been?)
3.Когда и почему он был там? (When and why has he been there?)
4.Где была его жена? (Where was his wife?)

EXERCISE 19

Listen to this song reading the text. Pay attention to the use of the past tense to make the conditional and the subjunctive by adding "бы". You can find the song on YouTube, the title is Если бы на Марсе были города" by the group Браво.

Если бы на Марсе были города
Я бы встал пораньше и слетал туда
Побродил по скверам рассмотрел дома
Если бы на Марсе были города

Я прошел бы дважды вдоль и поперек
С севера на запад с юга на восток
И возможно где-то повстречал тебя
Если бы на Марсе были города

На полчаса туда где ты носила белые банты
На полчаса туда где я был капитаном корабля
Туда где вечная весна на полчаса

Там осталось небо чистое как снег
Теплое как солнце яркое как свет

Длинные девчонки первая любовь
Жалко что на Марсе нет городов

На полчаса туда где ты носила белые банты
На полчаса туда где я был капитаном корабля
Туда где вечная весна на полчаса

Translation:
If on Mars there were cities
I would leave right away and fly there

211

Wandering on squares and watching the houses
If on Mars there were cities

I would passing by twice, far and wide, from North to West,
from South to East
and maybe somewhere I'd meet you
If on Mars there were cities

Half an hour and I'd get where you wore a white bow, half
an hour and I'd get where I was the captain of the ship,
where the spring is eternal in a half an hour

There is only the sky, pure like snow, warm like the sun,
strong like the light

Tall girls, first love
Unfortunately on Mars there are no cities

Half an hour and I'd get where you wore a white bow, half
an hour and I'd get where I was the captain of the ship,
where the spring is eternal in a half an hour

Let's disclose the secrets of this chapter

. In Russian there are not different past tenses, there is only one past tense.

. The Russian past works likewise an adjective: you have to consider the gender and the number of the subject.

. The Russian past tense is made by the infinitive of the verb without –ТЬ, and the suffixes -Л / -ЛА / -ЛО / -ЛИ for masculine, feminine, neuter or plural subject, following this order.

. Reflexive verbs follow the same rule: you have to add the particle СЯ at the end after the masculine past; after the other past forms you have to add СЬ.

. If you add the particle БЫ in the sentence, right before or after the verb in the past, this becomes subjunctive or conditional.

. You can make the hypothetical sentence with Если бы + past, past + бы.

ANSWERS.

Exercise 17

писать: писал — писала — писало - писали
курить: курил — курила — курило - курили
посещать: посещал — посещала — посещало - посещали
читать: читал — читала — читало - читали
петь: пел — пела — пело - пели
мыть: мыл — мыла — мыло - мыли
сидеть: сидел — сидела — сидело - сидели

учиться: учился — училась — училось - учились
улыбаться: улыбался —улыбалась — улыбалось - улыбались
смеяться: смеялся — смеялась — смеялось - смеялись
нравиться: нравился — нравилась — нравилось - нравились

Exercise 18

And have you ever been to the Kremlin before?

One of my friends has been living in Moscow for a year. I have not been here for too long instead. I asked him:

- Steve, can you show me Moscow landmarks? I think you have already seen everything here.

- I just know where my office and my house are. You know, I work all the time.

- I understand… I am sure you have been in the city center at least!

- Yes, I have been there. Yesterday a client from Tokyo and I were at the Kremlin and on the Red Square. My boss asked me to show it to him.

- Yesterday you saw the Red Square for the first time?!

- Yes. And the Kremlin too. You know, I didn't expect Moscow to be such a wonderful city!

- And where has your wife been in Moscow?

- А твоя жена где была в Москве?

- She has been at the mall "Moskva", at the store departments GUM and ZUM, at IKEA, at Stockmann, at Benetton, in the Pierre Cardin boutique. Yes, she has seen a lot in Moscow. And I realized it when I saw the bank statement.

Answers to questions:

1.Стив живёт в Москве.

2.Он уже был в Кремле и на Красной Площади.

3.Он был там вчера, потому что он это показал <u>клиенту</u> из Токио (dative).

4.Его жена была в универмаге "Москва", в ГУМе, в ЦУМе, в ИКЕЕ, в Стокманне, в Бенеттоне, в бутике "Пьер Карден".

DAY 18: DOING, KEEP DOING, FINISHING DOING

The chapter about the past tense was just a taste of a grammar apparently too good to be true.
Today we will focus in detail on the aspect of verbs.
Well, what is the *aspect*?

18.1. Expect the aspect

In Russian the majority of verbs is divided in two groups: an imperfective aspect (несовершенный вид, abbreviated more easily НСВ) and a perfective aspect (совершенный вид, СВ). The aspect of the verb determines the type of action. We do not have aspects in our language, since we just use modal verbs and the different verbal tenses.
Let's see right away an example to make the concept clear: compare these sentences

1. Вчера я читала книгу > verb читать, to read (НСВ, imperfective)
2. Вчера я прочитала книгу > verb прочитать, to read (СВ, perfective)

The verbs have the same meaning, "to read", but the concept of the action changes:
- in the **imperfective** form the action is continuous or generic
- in the **perfective** form the action is a precise point in the time, it happened and then concluded.

So, you could translate the two sentences in this way:

1. Yesterday I read a book.

2. 2. Yesterday <u>I finished reading</u> a book.

Another aspect that you have to keep in mind concerns the verbal tenses:

<u>imperfective:</u>
conjugation of the present tense= simple present
conjugation of the past tense= generic past tense, habitual or "continuous" (I have read, I was reading…)

<u>perfective:</u> (and here the situation is getting more complicated!)
conjugation of the present tense= **future tense**!!
conjugation of the past tense= past tense, accomplished, concluded (I read, I finished reading).

I know, this concept of the future could seem a grammatical cheap shot, but don't worry: we are going to study it in detail in the proper chapter (day 27).
For now, let's just try to better understand this concept of concluded action vs. action in development looking at some examples:
<u>Вчера</u> я **встал, позавтракал** и **прочитал** газету.
→ Vcherà yà vstal, pasàvtrakal i pracitàl gasiétu.
<u>Yesterday</u> I got up, I had breakfast and I read the newspaper. (all the actions concluded yesterday)

Когда я был маленьким, я <u>всегда</u> **играл** в футбол и **рисовал**.
→ Kagdà yà byl màlienkim yà vsiegdà igràl v futbòl.
When I was a child I <u>always</u> played soccer and I drew.

In the sentence there are some words that make you understand if the action is concluded or if it has a certain duration, as you can see underlined in the sentence.

The choice between imperfective/perfective depends on two fundamental aspects:
1. the context of the sentence;
2. the presence of "keywords" pointing out the type of action in its temporal duration. Take a look at some of them:

долго
регулярно
обычно
всегда
часто/редко
иногда
каждый день (каждый, каждую + accusative)
весь день (весь, всю, все + accusative)
2 дня
→ + **imperfective**

вдруг
сразу
наконѐц
за 2 дня
→ + **perfective**

18.2. Verbs playing in pairs

How do we distinguish a perfective verb from an imperfective one? You have to know that the peculiarity of these verbs is that they are paired. As we have seen in the first part with читать / прочитать, also the majority of verbs follow the same rule: the perfective aspect is made by adding prefixes to the perfective form. Prefixes can be various and they can have different meanings:

по- (a little, for a while, beginning of an action), до- (until something), у- (away, moving away), вы- (outside), в- (inside), ...

Not all imperfective verbs can have the perfective form with all the current prefixes (not always the combinations make sense!): for this reason it is necessary studying the aspects "in pairs". All the other forms with different prefixes are still perfectives, but among them there is always a "classic" one that matches its imperfective in the so-called "aspectual pair". Let's see some examples to understand it clearly:

Imperfective verbs   *Perfective verbs*

1. Adding prefixes to imperfective verbs

видеть *to see*	увидеть
готовить *to make*	приготовить
гулять *to walk*	погулять
делать *to do*	сделать
писать *to write*	написать
пить *to drink*	выпить
плакать *to cry*	заплакать
читать *to read*	прочитать

2. Vowel Alternation

встречать *to meet*	встретить

220

покупать *to buy*   купить
объяснять *to explain*   объяснить
получать *to receive*   получить
начинать *to start, to begin*   начать
понимать *to understand*   понять

Group of verbs with –нуть:
отдыхать *to rest*   отдохнуть
кричать *to shout, to scream*   крикнуть

Group of verbs with –ва-:
давать *to give*   дать
вставать *to get up*   встать
открывать *to open*   открыть
спрашивать *to ask (for something)*   спросить

3. Irregular verbs
брать *to catch*   взять
класть *to put, to lay*   положить
говорить *to talk, to say*   сказать
искать *to look for*   найти *to find*
ложиться *to go to sleep, to lie down*   лечь
становиться *to become*   стать
садиться *to sit down*   сесть

There are also some verbs that have only the imperfective aspect (they cannot have only the perfective one): in particular любить and работать. Think about it, you never stop loving… or working!

If you do not remember the perfective form, verbs like начинать/начать and заканчивать/закончить ("to start" and "to finish") can help you, since they are followed by the infinitive of the verb:

ex. Я читала, читала, читала и наконец **закончила читать** (= прочитала).
→ I read, read, read and finally I finished reading.

So, if you want to say that you finish working on Friday, you can say:
Я заканчиваю работать в пятницу.
Yà sakànchivaiu rabòtat' v piàtnizu.= I finish (always! it is in the imperfective form) working on Friday.

Attention: when you speak Russian with someone Russian, he/she could correct your use of imperfective/perfective, even if he/she perfectly understands what you are saying: do not get offended by this behaviour, but be grateful for that! In general Russians love giving advices and their point of view on a lot of matters, a personality trait that someone could find annoying. In my personal opinion I have always thought that it was useful, maybe one of the most useful lessons practicing Russian! I recommend to always accept willingly the advices and corrections of your way of speaking by a Russian: and who knows, maybe in the future you will thank him/her reciprocating.

Let's disclose the secrets of this chapter

. In the Russian language there is the concept of "aspect" of the verb: it is a peculiarity that specifies if the action of the verb is developping (repeatedly, habitually, continuous or generic) or if the action is concluded (finished in the past, a still point in the time).

. The two aspects of the Russian verb are the IMPERFEC-TIVE (action in development) and PERFECTIVE (concluded action) and they correspond to two different verbal forms.

. In general, the perfective form of a verb is made by adding prefixes to the imperfective form.

. For convenience, it is better to study the Russian verbs in "aspectual pairs" with the most common imperfective and perfective forms: ex. читать / прочитать.

. The imperfective aspect is used to make the simple present (an action in the present cannot be logically concluded). If the perfective verb is conjugated with the suffixes, then the verb changes in the future tense:
ex. делать / сделать = to do Я делаю = I do, я сделаю = I will do

. For us, understanding the concept of aspect of verbs is not easy: so, the help of a Russian mother tongue can be really fundamental.

DAY 19: TELL ME HOW YOU MOVE AND I WILL TELL YOU THE RIGHT VERB

Dear reader, get ready because this is the moment to deal with the archenemy of the Russian language. You surely noticed that, discussing about verbs, we never talked about the verb "**to go**". How come?

You have to know that, for some strange reason that I cannot understand, the Russian language built an entire and huge grammatical castle around the concept of "to go" and this castle is called "VERBS OF MOTION".

Believe me: if you overcome this lesson, Russian won't scare you anymore! Are you ready to tackle this adventure? Then, let's GO!

19.1. Even the verbs move

Yes, but how do we move? For the Russian language this question about "how" seems to be more important than "where". There are different verbs depending on the type of movement carried out by a subject.

In order to determine the right <u>verb of motion</u> you have to observe the action of the movement, the means with which the subject moves, the direction of the movement, and if the subject is possibly carrying objects.

The movement is "segmented" in little details that can help you understand which verb to use. So, if you look up the word "to go" in an English-Russian dictionary, you will find a very long headword; it is better knowing in advance how it works!

Tab. 10: THE MAIN VERBS OF MOTION AND THEIR MEANING (pay attention: they are all imperfectives)

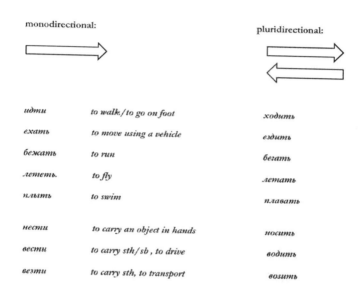

monodirectional:		pluridirectional:
идти	*to walk/to go on foot*	*ходить*
ехать	*to move using a vehicle*	*ездить*
бежать	*to run*	*бегать*
лететь.	*to fly*	*летать*
плыть	*to swim*	*плавать*
нести	*to carry an object in hands*	*носить*
вести	*to carry sth/sb, to drive*	*водить*
везти	*to carry sth, to transport*	*возить*

In the table you can see another division: in Russian there is also a distinction between a precise direction or more directions (back and forth, without a precise way, generic, etc.).
Pay attention: in this table I added only the *imperfective* verbs of motion, so the difference between monodirectional and pluridirectional verbs should not make you focus on the aspect. A verb of motion can have different meanings that enrich the sentence. Take a look at the differences between the two sentences:

идти в театр

ехать в театр

In English you would translate both sentences as "to go to the theater", but be careful because in the first one the meaning is "to walk/to go on foot", while in the second one

227

the verb ехать makes you understand that the theater is far away and you need a vehicle to reach it. Moreover, moving forward:

ходить в театр
ездить в театр

In this case also we are going to the theater but in the first sentence walking and in the second one by using a vehicle; in both cases it is not a one way, or it is a habitual action (for example we go to the theater every Saturday).

In order to understand the verbs of motion, you obviously need to recognize them inside the sentence and for this reason you have to know how to conjugate them.

For the pluridrectional verbs is easier (they are all verbs from the first and second group, see chapter 10), while the monodirectional ones work in a different way:

ИДТИ = to walk/to go on foot (monodirectional)- (the stress falls on the suffix)

иду
идёшь
идёт
идём
идёте
идут

ЕХАТЬ = to move by using a vehicle (monodirectional)- (the stress falls on the first E)

еду
едешь
едет
едем
едете
едут

Бежать = бегу, бежишь, бежит, бежим, бежите, бегут
Лететь = лечу, летишь, летит, летим, летите, летят
Плыть = плыву, плывёшь, плывёт ...

When the monodirectional verbs have the additional meaning "to carry" something or someone, they can give you a hard time (the pluridirectional ones are all from the second group – there is only the consonant alternation in the first person : я ношу – я вожу – я вожу):

НЕСТИ	**ВЕСТИ**	**ВЕЗТИ**
несу	веду	
везу		
несёшь	ведёшь	
везёшь		
несёт		
ведёт		везёт
несём		
ведём		везём
несёте		
ведёте		везёте
несут		
ведут		везут

(In these three verbs the accent always falls on the suffix)

EXERCISE 20

I know that right now this system could seem a little complicated and senseless to you, but it is really useful to understand instantly the meaning and the context of the sentence: try to translate the following sentences. The answers are at the end of the chapter.

1. Куда вы идёте?

Куда вы идёте? Мы идём домой. (Куда, kudà, means "where" as a motion toward a place)

2. Каждое утро школьники ходят в школу.
3. Мы едем в Россию.
4. Вы часто (often) ездите за границу (go abroad)
5. Корабли (ships) плывут в порт Одессы.
6. Мы плаваем в озере (lake).
7. Самолёты (airplanes) летят в аэропорт.
8. Птицы (birds) летают.
9. Спортсмены быстро бегают.
10. Я бегу на урок (to class).

EXERCISE 21

You need to practice to understand how нести/носить, вести/водить and везти/возить work, above all to understand what is the relation between the objects and the characters that describe the action. A classic exercise that you can find in the majority of Russian textbooks is describing an image. I suggest the same exercise with blank spaces where you have to put the correct verb of motion.

Pay attention, though because Russians make a difference between these two actions:

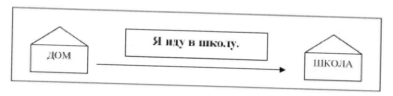

monodirectional motion

pluridirectional motion

Take a look at the image and complete the sentences:

Remember!
- monodirectional wants monodirectional;
- pluridirectional wants pluridirectional;
- in the sentence the two verbs are coherent on the direction.
Example:
1. Девушка _____ и _____ цветы.
    →идёт – несёт
The girl **walks** and she **carries** flowers in her hands.

2. Девушка _____ на мопеде и _____ цветы.
3. Мужчина _____ и _____ лощадь.
4. Люди _____ в музее.
5. Женщина _____ и _____ коробку.
6. Девушка _____ на велосипеде и _____ книги.
7. Мужчины _____ шкаф.
8. Человек _____ и _____ чемоданы.
9. Женщина _____ ‹
10. Человек _____ на мотоцикле и _____ собаку на коляске.
11. Человек _____ и _____ слона.
12. Девушка _____ и _____ цветы.
13. Женщины _____ и _____ детей.

A few words to understand the sentences:
девушка = girl
мужчина = man
лощадь = horse
люди = people
коробка = box
велосипед = bycicle
шкаф = closet
чемоданы = suitcases
девочка = little girl
мотоцикл = motorcycle
коляска = sidecar
слон = elephant
детей = (дети in the plural accusative, irr.) children

19.2. A useful scheme – not to go mad!

The verbs of motion are not over. Every student of Russian language at a certain point may think to have the capability to handle these verbs for a basic surviving: that is when the verbs of motion with the prefixes show up and then a new list of verbs of motion with new rules and meanings (to drag, to jump, to crawl, etc.). How do we survive? How can we not lose our mind?

Personally, I found a really useful method that I want to recommend: you should try keeping a notebook where you can write down just these verbs, all their strangenesses and peculiarities (in addition to the genaral scheme that we have seen earlier).
Consider the fact that, in the Russian daily life the verbs of motion are fundamental and if you get the verb wrong, some sentences could seem "impossible" to a Russian ; for example, if you ask for directions in a big city like Moscow you may hear a sentence like this:

Идти невозможно. Можно только ехать. (Itti nievasmòjna. Mòjna tòlka iéchat')
that means: It is impossible to walk there, you can reach it just by using a vehicle.

The long Russian distances are a great chance to practice with the verbs of motion, as we will see in the next chapter.

Another last important grammatical rule concerns the aspect: as we have already seen, the mono/pluri-directional duo is part of the imperfective aspect, pointing out an action in its development or continuity. There is also the **perfective** form of the verbs of motion and it is made <u>by adding the</u>

prefixes to the monodirectional form (and in the case of идти by slightly modifying the form of the verb):

идти – ходить (IMPERF.) →**пойти** (PERFECTIVE)
ехать – ездить →поехать
etc…

Attention! I went= я пошёл, yà pashòl, from **пойти**.
The other forms of the past tense are пошла, пошло and пошли.

Let's disclose the secrets of this chapter

. The verbs of motion are a vast and complex topic of the Russian language and it is better to tackle them by using schemes.

. In order to understand which verb of motion you have to use, you have to look at the movement in detail: direction, type of vehicle and possibly if the subject carries objects.

. The verbs of motion are divided into two groups: monodirectional and pluridirectional. The second type is also used to refer to habitual actions.

. The verbs of motion are conjugated like every other normal verb of first and second group. The monodirectional ones can give you a hard time.

. In order to make the perfective of the verbs of motion you have to add the prefixes to the monodirectional verb.

. Studying the verbs of motion is a continuous process: you have to dedicate yourself to it a lot!

ANSWERS.

Exercise 20
1. Where are you going? I go home.
2. Every morning the students go to school.
3. We go to Russia. (by a vehicle, not by walking!)
4. You often go abroad.
5. The ships enter the port of Odessa. (literally they swim!)
6. We swim in the lake.
7. The airplanes reach the airport. (literally they fly)
8. The birds fly. (toward different directions)
9. The athletes run fast. (generic activity)
10. I run to class. (a single direction)

Exercise 21
2. Девушка __едет__ на мотопеде и __везёт___ цветы.
3. Мужчина ___едет__ и ___везёт__ лощадь.
4.
5. Женщина ___идёт____ и ___несёт___ коробку.
6. Девушка _ездит_на велосипеде и ___возит____ книги.
7.Мужчины
8. Человек
9. Женщина
10.
11. Человек __идёт ____ и __ведёт_____ слона.
12. Девушка __идёт ___ и __везёт ___ цветы.
13. Женщины __ходят____ и ___возят __ детей.

DAY 20: LONG DISTANCES

We have already talked about how big Russia is, and since you have learned the verbs of motion, you can start describing your movements, inside or outside Russia.

A tour in the subway of Moscow is a real JOURNEY!

20.1. How to put into practice the verbs of motion

The verbs of motion must be used as much as possible to avoid to forget them, even if you get some of them wrong, you have to try anyway. Moreover, visiting a city like Moscow or Sain-Petersburg, or moving through the large Russian territory, sentences like "I have to go to…" or "how do I reach…?" can be really useful. Let's see some phases of a trip in Russia through the use of the verbs of motion in this brief text:

Я летел в Россию от Америки. Чемоданы пришли. Всё хорошо. Сейчас я еду на такси в город. Москва — огромный город: у него есть 12 (двенадцать) линий метро, очень много автобусов, троллейбусов и трамваев. На транспортом можно ездить только если у тебя есть билет. От гостинницы, я иду к остановке и потом еду на автобусе до станции метро "Маяковская". На метро сижу недолько: только две остановки и я уже пришёл в "Театральную". Там встречаю мою подругу Соня и мы вместе идём в театре.

(I got to Russia with a flight from the United States. Our suitcases arrived without any problems. Now I am going to the city by taxi. Moscow is a huge city: it has 12 underground lines and a lot of buses, trolley buses and tram. You can use the means of transport just if you have a ticket. From the hotel, I reach the bus stop and then I get to the underground station "Mayakovskaya". I do not stay so long on the train: only two stops and I reached "Teatralnaya". There, I meet with my friend Sonja and together we go to the theater).

You can see from the translation that the meaning match between the Russian verbs of motion and the English is never precise and linear. For example, летел: in Russian we cannot say "I flew to Russia from the United States", we have to find a similar expression. On the contrary, to a Russian, that simple verb летел (from лететь) bears more than one meaning: the movement toward a single direction (from the United States to Russia) and the means (by airplane). In the text, there is also a mix of verbal tenses and different verbs of motion, both mono or pluridirectional. There are also a lot of names of the means that you can use in the city:

ТРАНСПОРТ (trànspart) = public transportation

ВИДЫ ТРАНСПОРТА (vìdy trànsparta) = means of transport (ВИД stands for "means", but also "way")

ехать / ездить +		
на такси	na taksì	
на метро	na mietrò	
на автобусе	na avtòbusie	
на троллейбусе	na trallièibuse	
на трамвае	na tramvàie	
на велосипеде	na velosipiédie	
на мотоцикле	na motozìklie	
на мопеде	na mopiédie	= by scooter
на поезде	na pòesdie	= by train
на машине	na mashìnie	= by car

летать / лететь +		
на самолёте	na samaliòtie	= by airplane

плыть +		
на корабле	na karablié	= by ship
на пароходе	na parachòdie	= by ferry

<u>Remember:</u>

водить машину = to drive the car
идти пешком = to walk/ to go on foot (it strenghtens the concept of идти)
станция = underground station
остановка = tram, bus, trolley bus stop

20.2. Where are you going on holiday?

The holydays are a recent habit for Russians: during the Soviet era, tourism was just inside the country or in the areas belonging to the "satellite" countries. The opening at the end of the 80's brought a lot of social as well as political changes. In the last years, the spread of a major wealth among the population allowed the phenomenon of tourism to grow at a global level.

Unfortunately, not all parts of population can afford a holiday or long trips: one of the most favourite places perfect to relax is the dacha, especially during summer (see chapter 12). There are also some classic destinations in Russia and nearby: Сочи, Sochi, became famous in the last few years since it welcomed the Winter Olympics Games, but it is a seaside resort on the Black Sea, as Yalta and Odessa in Ukraine, famous for the thermal therapy (курорт).

Let's imagine hearing a conversation about holidays: the Nikitin family is deciding where to spend the summer, but dad, mom, Irina and Alësha have different ideas.

Ирина: Папа, скажи, какие у нас планы на отпуск в этом году?

Папа: Я решил ездить на Кавказ в Гагру. Это великолепный курорт в Абхазии. Он находится около Черного моря недалеко от Сочи. Погода там обычно чудесная, а вода в море теплая с мая по ноябрь.

Алёша: Но папа! Курорт – это скучно! Мы с Ириной хотели бы ездить за границу... в Испанию!

Мама: В Испанию? Там ужасно! Слишком жарко! А я думала о Сибире, именно о Байкале: как вы думаете, кемпинг около озера? Прекрасно!

Ирина, Алёша: УЖАСНО, мама!

Папа: Дети, не говорите таким образом маме. А ты, мылая, уже знаешь, что мы не любим кемпинг.

Ирина: Папа, делаем так: мы вместе едем в Испанию, а потом вы с мамой летите обратно в Россию и едете на Кавказ или на Байкал, как вы хотите...
Мама: Ирина, ты знаешь, что это невозможно!
Папа: ...и <u>денег не хватают</u>!

Translation:
Irina: Dad, tell us, what are our <u>holydays</u> plans this year?
Dad: I have decided to go to the Caucasus region, to Gagra: it is a beautiful thermal place in Abkhazia. It is nearby the Black Sea and not so far away from Sochi. The climate is wonderful and the water is warm from May to November.
Alësha: Dad, c'mon! The <u>thermal baths</u> are so boring! Irina and me would like to go <u>abroad</u>... to Spain!
Mom: Spain? But it is terrible there! Too hot! I was thinking about Siberia, the Bajkal lake: what about a <u>camping</u> by the lake? Nice!
Irina, Alësha: That's terrible mom!
Dad: Guys, don't use that tone with your mom. And you, my dear, you know that we don't love camping.
Irina: Dad, what about this: we go all together to Spain, and then you and mom come back to Russia, to the Caucasus or to the Bajkal lake, as you wish...
Mom: Irina, you know that it is impossible!
Dad: ... and <u>the money wouldn't be enough</u>!

Read again this dialogue and take a look at the cases with the prepositions: here a list of the main prepositions of place that can be useful to orient yourself in the space.

Tab. 11: PREPOSITIONS OF PLACE AND GOVERNMENTS

около/ недалеко от/ близко= nearby, close by	
далеко= far away	
от...до= from...to/until...	+GENITIVE
у=by	
из/с= from	

в/на= in, inside	+ PREPOSITIONAL

в/на= towards, to (movement towards a place)	
за= beyond	+ACCUSATIVE
через= through	

к= towards (moving closer to sth/sb)	+DATIVE
по= through, by	

And you? Where do you want to go for your next holidays?

ОТПУСК – ГДЕ? (where, name of the place, without any movement)
на море
в горах
на озере

на деревне
в городе
за границей

ОТПУСК – КУДА? (where to, movement toward a place)
на море
в горы
на озеро
на деревню
в город
за границу
В этом году хочу отдыхать…
V ètamgadù ià chaciù addykhàt' v…

Although its hard sound, the verb отдыхать means "to relax", "to spend the holidays". More precisely, отпуск means "vacation", "day off".

In the next few years, in Russia, tourism could develop more and more, and who knows, maybe this lesson could come in handy soon!

Let's disclose the secrets of this chapter

. The Russian verbs of motion are used in the daily life.

. A verb of motion can have multiple meanings in comparison with English: usually you have to translate them by using longer expressions.

. In the largest cities, the choice between the public transport is vast and they are spread all over the territory.

. The holydays abroad are a recent phenomenon for Russians, derived from the economic development of the last years.

. There are various prepositions to specify the place, and each is governed by a case. The genitive is the most used case, together with the prepositions of place.

. The questions ГДЕ and КУДА both mean "Where?": the first one specifies the place (where is placed sth), the second one specifies a movement toward a place (where are you heading to?).

DAY 21: BETWEEN FAIRY TALE AND NOVEL

So, you finished your third week of study of Russian: I have to admit that it was not a piece of cake. The verbs of motion, a real grammatical cheap shot! As I said, though, if you survive this, you can survive everything! Today I suggest a more recreational theme that will get you closer to this interesting and ancient culture.

Here an original version of the famous cartoon "Masha and the Bear".

21.1. Learning Russian by reading

The most precious advice that I have ever received during the study of Russian was reading books about Russia. It may seem commonplace, but ,in our everyday life, everything concerning Russia rarely peeks out in a spontaneous way, unless we look for it.

I think that it is right and proper for everyone interested in a language showing interest for its culture too: otherwise, the study would be just about repeating formulas and schemes and it would be even harder.

That is why today I would like talking about some Russian books that, I think, cannot absolutely be missed in your bookshelf:

- Russian fairy tales: they are incredibly full of meanings and also fundamental to understand the deepest roots of the culture of every people, and in Russia fairy tales are so important. In the editions that you can find in the open-air markets or in the bookstores in Russia, there are a lot beautiful and "traditional" drawings. Reading them in Russian could be a useful exercise, since the text is often repetitive and in the form of a song or a poem, even if some words are archaic and by now not used anymore. A lot of tales start with the sentence Жили-были старик и старуха..., meaning "Once upon a time there were an old man and an old lady...".

- the greatest novels of the 19th century: part of the general culture, often forgotten, includes stories that cannot be missed in the cultural heritage of a Russian lover. In general, they are not so easy to read nor to deal with: often they are about historians living in a specific era that we do not know

so well. However, the satisfaction and also the melancholy that you will feel leafing through the last page of one of these novels are unique feelings that you have to experience at least once in your life.
You cannot miss: Anna Karenina by Tolstoy and Crime and Punishment by Dostoevsky. But I'd be wrong recommending you just these two masterpieces.

-short stories: it is easier to deal with them in comparison with the great novels (and they are lighter to carry too!), but you should not underrate them. Both Tolstoy and Dostoevsky have dealt with this genre, such as other writers. You absolutely have to read The Nose and The Overcoat by Gogol.

- the twentieth-century novels and autobiographies: the historical impact of the 20th century on Russia is described in a realistic way by Pasternak, in his Doctor Zhivago (in Russian there is a Ж, Живаго, so do not pronounce it as a "z"!) and also in a more dreamlike way, but equally successful, by Bulgakov in his The Master and Margarita. These are books that should be read with the support of an introduction and a good literary critique, since it is not so easy to understand them right away, but without any doubts, they leave an unforgettable trace in everyone's literary imagination.

- poetry and theater: Pushkin, Chekhov, Mayakovskij... There are a lot of Russian names linked to poetry and in general to theater. This last one is even more beautiful if you have the chance to see it in first person: The Cherry Orchard by Chekhov is a real gem.

- essays: maybe this is the most useful part, placed side by side with the proper reading, not to get lost and to better understand the context of the reading. Talking about this genre, a really unique book is **Natasha's Dance** by Orlando Figes, a book about the Russian history from its origin to the modern age, interpreting it from a cultural and artistic point of view, as well as historical, in a fluid way and also so pleasant to read.

These are just a few recommendations and I know that the we do not have enough time to dedicate to reading, but if you are at this point (and you overtook the quick sands of the verbs of motion!) it means that you are a determined reader and you always want to knowmore and more. I think reading is the best way to do that, isn't it?

21.2. Cult characters

Typical characters that became part of the collective imagination come from the Russian literature and culture. A lot of them derive from the fairy tales and legends that we talked about earlier:

- **Баба Яга**, Bàba Yagà: more cruel than the witch of Snow White and with creepy intents similar to those of the witch of Hansel and Gretel, Baba Yaga is a typical character of a lot of fairy tales for children. She flies riding a mortar, she erases paths in the woods, and she lives in a "mobile" home placed on chicken feet, waiting for some unlucky person to enslave (or to cook directly in the oven). Baba Yaga is like the Bogeyman, Russian kids are told "If you behave badly, Baba Yaga is coming after you!"(Будешь плохо себя вести - Баба Яга заберёт).

- **the bogatytry** Iliya Muromec, Alësha Popovich and Dobryniya Nikitich: heroic warriors belonging to the Russian tradition (or more in general to the Slavic one), famous for their great endeavours and celebrated in the national Medieval poems. Each one of them represents a virtue or a peculiar quality that glorify the mythological figure: Iliya Muromec for his greatness and strength, Alësha Popovich as a symbol of shrewdness and intelligence, Dobryniya Nikitich represented as a typical kind hero. These knights are not just a literary subject, but they are also represented in paintings (for example the paintings by Viktor Vasnetsov are famous).

- **Дед Мороз и Снегурочка**, that is to say Grandfather Frost and Snegurochka. In the Western tradition we are used to the idea that Santa Claus brings the gifts under the tree; in the Slavic tradition, this task is carried out by Grandfather

Frost and his assistant and nephew (daughter according to other versions), Sniégurachka, literally "small snow".

Nowadays, we have a major access to the Russian culture in comparison with the past, and for this reason another famous duo from the fairy tales world is also on tv: we are talking about **Маша и Медведь**, Masha and the Bear, the famous cartoon for kids! Kids love it for its simplicity and adults for its tranquillity, you will love it too and you cana use ite as a funny tool to listen to a Russian and follow Masha and her friend the Bear's adventures. Speaking of this cartoon: in the original version, the bear is not so nice. But Masha is a clever little girl and she finds a way to get by even in the most difficult situations.

So, fairy tales never let us down!

Let's disclose the secrets of this chapter

. You can alternate the study of the language with the reading of something "Russian".

. You do not have to launch yourself in the original Russian texts: a first reading in your language is really useful as well as enjoyable.

. Fairy tales are a gold mine from which you can better understand the popular Russian culture.

. Besides the literary classic genres, never forget to leave space to essays too: they are really useful to understand deeply wht you are reading and how you should read it.

. The Russian culture is full of "cult" characters that entered the collective imagination: the most symbolic ones come from fairy tales.

. You can have fun watching Masha and the Bear in the original Russian version: there are not great dialogues, but it is really intuitive and some scenes are so brilliant! Every now and then we deserve relax!

DAY 22: COUNT ON ME

You have surely noticed that we have not talked about numbers yet. As in many languages, in Russian too, numbers are a peculiar topic: they are not nouns nor proper adjectives. It is not so hard to learn them, especially if you have to list them to count.

22.1. Innumerable numbers

Now, let's see how numbers from one to twenty work, and then the main rules:

0 ноль
1 один / одна / одно (depending on the gender); when Russians count, they say "раз"
2 два / две (masc. or fem.)
3 три (starting from this point, there is no distinction concerning the gender).
4 четыре
5 пять
6 шесть
7 семь
8 восемь
9 девять
10 десять

Now repeat: adìn, dvà, tri, cetìrie, pyàt', shést', siém', vòsiem', diévyat', diésyat'

Pay attention: from the five on, all numbers end with the soft sign. On the contrary, until four they follow a different scheme (with the exception of zero that we leave apart). Keep in mind this distinction as we move on to the next paragraph.

From ten to twenty, numbers follow a precise construction scheme:

number without ь + над (on, over) + цать (abbreviated form of десять)
so, literally "1 above ten"= eleven.

11 одиннадцать	adìnnazzat'
12 двенадцать	dvienàzzat'
13 тринадцать	trinàzzat'
14 четырнадцать	cetyrnazzat'
15 пятнадцать	pidnàzzat'
16 шестнадцать	shestnàzzat'
17 семнадцать	simnàzzat'
18 восемнадцать	vasimnàzzat'
19 девятнадцать	dieviatnàzzat'
20 двадцать	dvàzzat'

As you have seen, this second group of numbers are really long nouns and their pronunciation is affected by this fact simplyfying where it is possible reducing some letters, as in пятнадцать that becomes *pidnàzzat'*.

From twenty on, numbers are built such as in English:
21 двадцатьодин/ одна / одно
22 двадцатьдва / две
23 двадцатьтри
...
30 тридцать
31 тридцать один
...
40 сорок (sòrak, the only one outside of the box: it derives from the name of an ancient unit of measurement)
41 сорок один/ одна / одно
...

And from fifty on, even the tens follow a precise scheme:
number with ь + десят

50 пятьдесят	pidisiàt
60 шестьдесят	shésdisiat
70 семьдесят	siémdisiat
80 восемьдесят	vòsiemdisiat

The closer you get to 100 and more strangenesses you will find:

90 девяноста	divianòsta
100 сто	stò

Here some big numbers that can come in handy for example to pay the bill at the restaurant: you do not have to spend to the last penny, but now the number has three zero:

200 двести	dviésti
300 триста	trìsta
400 четыреста	cety'riesta

And as we have seen, from five on the same scheme: number + сот

500 пятьсот	pitsòt
600 шестьсот	shessòt
700 семьсот	simsòt
800 восемьсот	vasimsòt
900 девятьсот	diviatsòt
1000 тысяча (Russians pronounce it тыша)	tìsiacha

At this point, you can already start composing numbers: for example, 1256 is тысяча двести-пятьдесятшесть.
Russians pronounce numbers really quickly at a first listening: more than once I remember I didn't utter a word in front of the cashier at the supermarket; then I learnt to get by by observing the price on the screen of the register! You cannot say that the cashiers care about the fact that you do

not understand Russian: we can just say that they do not like repeating the same sentences everytime, since they already have a repetitive job.

Тысяча рублей (1000 roubles) have not a great purchasing power as it seems: right now one pound is worth about 98 roubles, and so, besides a dinner in a restaurant (a cheap one), you cannot afford so much.

So, let's see what happens after 1000:
2000 две тысячи
3000 три тысячи
4000 четыре тысячи

5000 пять тысяч
6000 шесть тысяч
...
10.000 десять тысяч
100.000 сто тысяч
1.000.000 миллион
1.000.000.000 миллиард

Now you are well trained, so you can face numbers like 1.342.678.900:
миллиард триста сорок два миллиона шестьсот семьдесят восемь тысяч девятьсот

one billion three hundred forty-two million six hundred seventy-eight thousands nine hundred

Let's get it started!

EXERCISE 22

How would you pronounce these numbers in Russian?
(The answers at the end of the chapter)

12 _____

37 _____

65 _____

99 _____

134 _____

569 _____

801 _____

1048 _____

2306 _____

3500 _____

7040 _____

10.866 _____

44.333 _____

1.999.303 _____

22.2. Numbers make jokes

You surely have noticed that the numbers one, two, three and four are a special group in comparison with the others, for their structure and for how they work. Let's set aside "one" that works as an adjective, and let's focus on the others.

Until now, we have seen how numbers work on their own, without being linked to a noun; but, when we use them to enumerate something, they are followed by the genitive case. For example, let's see what happens if I want to say "three girls":

три девушки
number + singular genitive

So, if we count the girls, we would say:

одна девушка (one wants the normal nominative, clearly in the right gender)
две девушки (number in the feminine form)
три девушки
четыре девушки

Until this point, everything seems to be fine. But, as I said, two-three-four are a special group that follows specific rules. From five on something happens:

пять девушек
шесть девушек
семь девушек
восемь девушек
...

With the numbers from five on, you have to use the genitive in the plural form, a case with a lot of variants: in the case of девушка, feminine noun, the plural genitive should be *девушк, without the final vowel, but, since it becomes un-pronounceable, a "e" is added between the two last consonants: девушек.

Be careful, though: numbers like 22, 23, 24, 32, 33, 34, etc. follow the scheme of the group two-three-four and they are followed by the singular genitive.
So, be ready when the numbers start joking!

EXERCISE 23

Complete the sentences with the singular or plural genitive of the nouns depending on the numbers. Remember: "one" wants the nominative!

1. человек: sing. gen. человека – plural genitive людей (person/people)

два .....

три ......

семь....

2. ребёнок: sing. gen. ребёнка – plural gen. детей (child/children)

восемнадцать....

четыре...

один .....

3.собака: sing. gen. собаки – plural gen. собак (dog/dogs)

три ......

десять...

одна .....

4. рубль: sing. gen. рубля – plural gen. рублей (rouble/roubles)

двадцать четыре .....

сто сорок ......

тысячи девятьсот трдцать один .....

5. дом: sing. gen. дома – plural gen. домов (house/houses)

сорок четыре .....

сто двадцать два ....

две тысячи...

Let's disclose the secrets of this chapter

.Learning the numbers in order to count is easy.

. From one to ten numbers are easy e not so different from ours. "One" has all three genders, "two" has masculine and feminine, the others have no gender.

. All the numbers from five to ten end with the soft sign.

. To make the numbers from 11 to 20, you just have to add -надцать after the basic number, removing the soft sign if they have it: ex. три →тринадцать, 13.

. To make the tens from 50 to 80 you just have to add -десят at the end of the basic number, this time keeping the soft sign: ex. семь →семьдесят, 70.

. The numbers two, three and four are followed by the singular genitive of the noun that they refer to. "One" wants the nominative. The other numbers want the plural genitive. You have always to take a look at the final numberin order to understand which case to use after (this is not valid for 12, 13 and 14, that want the plural genitive).

ANSWERS.

Exercise 22

12 = двенадцать
37 = тридцать семь
65 = шестьдесят пять
99 = девяноста девять
134 = сто тридцать четыре
569 = пятьсот шестьдесят девять
801 = восемьсот один
1048 = тысяча сорок восемь
2306 = две тысячи триста шесть
3500 = три тысячи пятьсот
7040 = семь тысяч сорок
10.866 = десять тысяч восемьсот шестьдесят шесть
44.333 = сорок четыре тысяча триста тридцать три
620.507 = шестьсот двадцать тысяч пятьсот семь
1.999.303 = миллион девятьсот девяноста девять тысяч триста три

Exercise 23

1. два человека (2); три человека (3); семь людей (7)
2. восемнадцать детей (18); четыре ребёнка (4); один ребёнок (1)
3. три собаки (3); десять собак (10); однасобака (1)
4. двадцать четыререубля (24); сто сорокрублей (140); тысячи девятьсот трдцать один рубль (1931)
5. сорок четыредома (44); сто двадцать двадома (122); две тысячи домов (2000)

DAY 23: IT IS TIME TO TALK ABOUT TIME

We have already talked about the concept of time for Russians, but we have not talked about how to say what time is it. The system is not so different from ours and it is easy to memorize.

23.1. How to read a clock

As in English, we consider the clock divided in two parts: the first one that goes from 12 to half hour, and the second one from the 30 minutes to the next hour.

In order to express the time, you have to use the ordinal numbers that work as adjectives.

первый	piérvyi
второй	vtaròi
третий	triétii *(the only one that has a soft declension!)*
четвёртый	cetviòrtyi
пятый	piàtyi
шестой	shestòi
седьмой	siedmòi
восьмой	vas'mòi
девятый	deviàtyi
десятый	desiàtyi
одиннадцатый	adìnnazzatyi
двенадцатый	dvienàzzatyi

and for the minutes you just have to remember the numbers that we have already studied at chapter five, adding some terms:

ровно = on the dot
четверть = a quarter
пол- / половина = half → полчаса = half hour
без = to

268

Прошло четверть часа   **Прошло полчаса**   **Прошёл час**

If you want to know the time, you have to ask the question Который час? (katòryi ciàs), meaning "what time is it?"(the verb "to be" is invisible in the sentence as always). When it comes to answer, you have to think like a Russian: a quarter past 2 means, from a Russian point of view, a quarter past the third hour of the day (the one that goes from 2 to 3):
ex. What time is it? It is a quarter past two
→ Который час? Четвертъ третъего. (of the third hour= genitive of the ordinal)

Let's see how to express all the hours in the first half of the clock:
7:00 ровно семь
7:05 пять минут восьмого
7:10 десять минут восьмого
7:15 четвертъ восьмого (пятнадцать минут восьмого)
7:20 двадцать минут восьмого
7:25 двадцать пять минут восьмого
7:30 полвосьмого

Be careful, though: the eighth hour of the day (восьмого) is the one that goes from 7 to 8. Listening to the hours in Russian, you can risk to be mistaken and you would count an hour forward.

In the other part of the clock, after the half hour, you have to use another word, без (biés):

7:40 без двадцати восемь
7:45 без четверти восемь
7:50 без десяти восемь
7:55 без пяти восемь

The sentence with без has a peculiar structure: без is always followed by the GENITIVE of the number (oh yes, numbers must be declined too!), that is made by adding a И, and the the nominative of the number of the next hour.

ex. a quarter to four= без четверти четыре.

So, differently from what we are used to, the most "difficult" part is the first half, where you have to remember that Russians are always a step forward, and for this reason they do not say "it is two o'clock" but "the third hour", or "it is three o'clock" becomes "the fourth hour" and so on.

Полдень = midday, noon
Полночь = midnight

The time is expressed through numbers until 12 and if it is necessary, you have to specify the moment of the day: утра (morning), дня (daytime, afternoon), вечера (evening), ночи (night).
In the official schedules (airports, stations...), the time is read in full.

EXERCISE 24

What time is it? Write in Russian the time. Answers at the end of the chapter.

16:15_____

09:55_____

07:00_____

18:05_____

04:20_____

And now the opposite exercise:

без четверти четыре_____

пять минут девятого_____

полпервого_____

без пяти семь _____

четверть седьмого _____

23.2. What time did it happen?

Answering to someone who wants to know the time (and you could use the good old trick of showing the clock to the passer-by showing off your best smile!) is different from asking "At what time" you do something.

В котором часу? =At what time?
Когда? = When?

In order to answer, you have to use the preposition В followed by the time as you have already seen earlier.
Ex. Когда вы его встретили вчера? В шесть часов вечера.
(at 6 p.m.)

All the constructions with без do not change, they do not need В in addition, while половина must be in the prepositional case: в половине седьмого= half past six
Lastly, the ordinal numbers that you have learned for the time can come in handy for the dates: if you want to say that something happened in a specific year, the number is not enough:

Example:

in 1994= в тысяча девятьсот девяноста четвёртом году

The last number is an ordinal numeral adjective like the ones of the time and it must be declined in the prepositional case (followed by году, gadù, meaning year).

If you want to express time in other ways, come back to the chapter 11 where we have talked about days and months. The date can be expressed in three ways: to remember the structure, use a date reference such as your birthday or a special event and remember it in the three cases:

1. В + year in the PREPOSITIONAL case
ex. в две тысячи шестнадцатом году = in 2016

2. В + month in PREPOSITIONAL case + year in GENITIVE case
ex. в мае тысяча девятьсот шестьдесят восьмого года = in May 1968

3. day in GENITIVE case + month in GENITIVE case + year in GENITIVE case
ex. десятого августа тысяча девятьсот девяноста первого года

Let's disclose the secrets of this chapter

. In order to learn the time in Russian, divide the clock in two halves: in each one there is a specific rule.

. To express time you need the ordinal numerals, adjectives formed by the number, all in hard declension, except "third" (третий) that follows the soft declension.

. In the first half of the clock, you have to say the minutes and then the ordinal numeral in the genitive case. Remember: a quarte past two is "fifteen minutes of the third hour".

. In the second half of the clock you have to use без + genitive of the minutes to express how many minutes to the next hour, expressed in nominative case.

. If you have to answer to the question "at what time?"use в + the hour in accusative case

. There are three ways to express the date. The last number indicating the year is declined in the prepositional or genitive case depending on how the date is expressed.

ANSWERS.

Exercise 24
16:15 четверть пятого
09:55 без пяти десять
07:00 семь часов
18:05 пять минут седьмого вечера
04:20 двадцать минут пятого утра

And now the opposite exercise:
без четверти четыре →03:45
пять минут десятого →09:05
полпервого → 12:30
без пяти семь →06:55
четверть седьмого →06:15

DAY 24: LET'S GO SHOPPING

During a vacation in Russia, besides the visits in the museums, the long walks in the parks and lunches and dinners in restaurants, good shopping cannot be missed. Be careful men, I'm talking to you too!
In the last years Russia opened to the global market and the traces of some kind of consumerism are visible above all in the largest cities: there are plenty of malls, and as a perfect cliché, on Sundays there is always a long line on the highway to the exit of Ikea (once I almost lost my flight to go there!).

A good part of the consumption of Russians is going toward the luxury goods, and Moscow is a gold mine when it comes to find them. Sometimes, though, the results of this consumerism are a little too gaudy or terribly exaggerated (for example, the pink Hummer limousine parked in front of clubs). Moreover, recently a new social category appeared, the so-called new Russians (новые русские).
Today we fly low and if possible, without spending too much roubles and imagining a shopping evening in a Russian city like Moscow.

24.1. Let's dress in layers

So, clearly, the first thing that comes in your mind when you are about to leave to Russia is your suitcase: big or small? A lot or a few clothes? Which summer clothes and which winter ones? The solution, as it is for everywhere, is thinking about dressing in layers. This is useful above all for the winter, but also for summer: for example, August is a continuous slide toward fall and if it begins with scorching temperatures, it can end forcing you to wear a coat.

Leave putting in your suitcase different clothes, but keep in mind the layers: as we have seen, during winter, in pubs or inside the houses the heating is really high (the same thing happens during summer with the air conditioning!). So, how do we pack the suitcase? Let's make a list to avoid to forget something:

ОДЕЖДА= clothes (collective noun)

- бельё= underwear
- пижама = pyjamas
- носки или колготки = tights or pantyhose (you can also find леггинсы!)
- пальто, куртка или анорак = overcoat, jacket or windbreaker
- плащ = raincoat
- тёплые свитеры = warm sweaters
- джинсы или брюки = jeans or trousers
- футбольки = t-shirts
- рубашка / блузка = shirt/ blouse (men/women)
- костьюм / платье = suit/dress (men/women)
- перчатки или варежки = gloves (the first term indicates the gloves with the separated fingers, in leather; the second one indicates the wool gloves like mittens)
- шапка = hat

- шарф = scarf
- стойкие ботинки, сапоги, или кроссовки= shoes, boots or sneakers.

If you happen to go to Russia during summer, do not forget a купальный костюм or a бикини, together with сандалы and солнечные очки (sunglasses).

Once in Russia, you will surely realize you have forgotten something, but don't worry: as my mom always says, "shops are evrywhere" and in our case, you just have to learn what to say once inside one of them!

24.2. What to do in a shop

The shop assistants not necessarily might be smiling or being willing: it depends on the brand they work for, but also on the cultural aspect connected to the smile, that we have already seen at the beginning, (a Russian thinks: "I am working, why should I be smiling?"). Do not let this unpleasent behavior intimidate you and ask for their help if you need it.

Take a look at this dialogue between продавщица (shop assistant) and а клиент (client).
продавщица: Здравствуйте! Я могу Вам помочь? *shop assistant: Hi! Can I help you?*
клиент: Пока нет, спасибо. Я просто смотрю. *client: Not for now. I am just taking a look.*

Later...

к.: Покажите, пожалуйста, вот эти джинсы. *client: Can you show me those jeans, please?*
п.: Сейчас принесу. *Shop assistant: I am getting them.*
к.: Сколько они стоят? *Client: How much is it?*
п.: Три тысячи рублей *shop assistant: 3000 roubles*
к.: Спасибо. Где я могу их примерить? *client: Thanks. Where can I try them?*

п.: Примерочная находится в конце зала. *Shop assistant: The fitting rooms are at the end of the room.*
к.: Спасибо. *Client: Thanks.*

After a couple minutes:

п.: Вам подошли джинсы? *shop assistant: Do the jeans fit you?*
к.: Да. Я их беру! *client: Yes. I am taking them!*

The underlined key passages in the dialogue are also the sentences that can come in handy in a shop (a clothing shop or something else):

- Покажите, пожалуйста ... = can you show me (in Russian it is an imperative)
- Где я могу их примерить? = where can I try them?
- Сколько стоит / стоят? = how much is it/ are they?

Lastly, a very useful word that I underlined in the dialogue is the verb находиться (nakhòdizza), *to be*. The question is "Где находится ... ?" can be useful in a lot of contexts.

Once you have chosen what to buy you can go to the касса and платить, *to pay*.

Besides the various shops, the Russian cities have a strong tradition for what concerns kiosks, stands and markets that sell every kind of product. You surely have to visit them if you want to buy Russian souvenirs at a fair price, but also if you want to try to negotiate on prices, a tradition belonging to their culture.
There are not precise sentences to do that, nor all sellers are always willing to accept your requests, but you can always try to lower the price that you were proposed with simple attempts like:

Давайте, на сто! = c'mon, let's do 100 roubles
Нет, слишком дорогой = no, it's too expensive
У меня только сто рублей = I just have 100 roubles

Often, a well acted attempt is enough to persuade the seller, and it could also entertain him!
A really traditional place where to practice this art, is the Вернисаж in Izmailovo, in the North area of Moscow, nearby the underground station Partizanskaja: besides its ar-

chitecture, a sort of wooden kremlin where you can find many stands inside, it is also interesting taking a look at all types of products there. As a matter of fact, in addition to traditional Russian souvenirs (matryoshka dolls, carillon, wooden or wool objects, fur hats, painted boxes, amber jewels and fairy tales books), you can also find unique objects from the Soviet era (infinite medals, watches and more or less original objects belonging to the military world or to the factories) and traces of the Tsarist past dating back to the first years of the 20th century.

Bringing back home a piece of Russia has never been so easy. But be careful: always try to negotiate!
Besides making the seller happy, taking on a negotiation that could become a funny one, you could also take advantage of a good discount.

Let's disclose the secrets of this chapter

. During a trip in Russia, shopping cannot be missed.

. With the consumerism, the largest Russian cities have become similar to the other Western cities, with the shops of the major brands and also with various shop chains.

. When you pack your suitcase for a trip to Russia, whatever season, consider to dress in layers.

. If you forget something, don't worry: shops are everywhere, and in the Russian shops you can find everything. You just need some set phrases.

. Walking between the stands of a market is an experience that cannot be missed in your trip to Russia.

. When it comes to souvenirs, a lot of sellers love to negotiate: you can try some simples phrases or relying on being fun.

DAY 25: HOTFOOT!

It may seem incredible, but a language like Russian that divides the movement in little details and uses a lot of verbs to express it, has not so much words to refer to the parts of the human body.

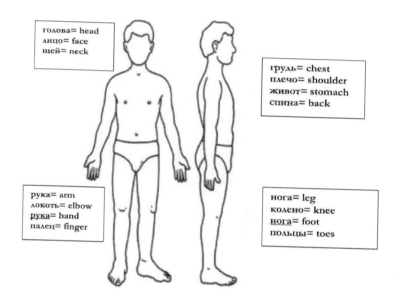

голова= head
лицо= face
щей= neck

грудь= chest
плечо= shoulder
живот= stomach
спина= back

рука= arm
локоть= elbow
рука= hand
палец= finger

нога= leg
колено= knee
нога= foot
польцы= toes

25.1. A lot of parts, a few names

Sometimes, associating the words to an illustration is a good method to memorize them. Let's try it with the parts of the human body in Russian:

голова = head (galavà)
лицо = face (lizò)
щей = neck (scièi)

грудь = chest (grud')
плечо = shoulder (pliecò)
живот = stomach (jivòt)
спина = back(spinà)

рука = arm and forearm (rukà)
локотъ = elbow(lakòt')

рука = hand (rukà)
палец = finger (pàliez)

нога = leg (nagà)
колено = knee(kalienò)
нога = foot (nagà)
пальцы = toes (pàlzy – in the declension, the "e" of the singular disappears)

You have surely noticed that the arm and the leg, until the hand and the foot included, are translated with рука (rukà) and нога (nagà): pretty convenient if you think about it!
Obviously, there are specific terms for all parts of the body, but they are not so common. In the speech, everything is semplified and the context helps you understand if someone is talking about a hand or an arm.

Observing in detail, let's see also the parts of the face (I will write the pronunciation just if it is uncertain):

лоб = forehead
бровь = eyebrow глаза = eyes (glasà)
ухо (plural: уши)= ear нос = nose
щека = cheek(shikà)
рот = mouth
губы = lips
зубы = teeth
подбородок = chin (padbaròdak)
борода = beard (baradà)
усы = moustache
волосы = hair (vòlasi)

In the collective imagination, a Russian has this type of face:
светлые волосы, синие глаза, маленький нос
(fair hair, blue eyes, small nose)

...but there are a lot of variants! Let's see some adjectives for eyes and hair:

глаза:
синие = blue
зелёные = green
серые = gray
карие = brown
чёрные = black
фиолетовые = violet
маленькие = small
большие = big

287

волосы:
светлые = fair
рыжие = red
русые = blonde, light chestnut-brown
каштановый = chestnut-brown
чёрные = black
серые = gray
прямые = straight
кудрявые = curly
длинные = long
короткие = short

In Russia, a lot of people have fair hair and you can notice it passing by the hair dye section: it is impressive seeing all those hair dyes for chestnut-brown or red and a few ones for the blonde!

Do not forget that Russia is huge and the people living in this country have different physical traits: in the Eastern area, it is not rare finding physical traits typical of the Far Eastern zone, like almond-shaped eyes and super straight hair, and the same in the South area, in the Caucasus region, you can find more Mediterranean traits.
As we have always said, Russia is a big country and its diversity is a quality to find out.

25.2. It hurts right here...

Let's admit it, sooner or later, we all get sick, and as tourists in Russia, the reasons can be mainly two: cold and... alcohol!

In the first case, the consequences can be a cold or a flu or a general illness. In this context, it could be useful some expressions:

in general, if you want to say that you feel pain in some parts of your body, you say:

у меня болит + singular subject
у меня болят + plural subject

ex.   у меня болит голова – u minià bòlit galavà
        у меня болит зубы – u minià bòlit sùby

In the second case, Russians use some unusual treatments against the hangover (похмелье): some people recommend drinking a beer in the morning, and others a big glass of pickle juice.

Russians love giving advices and often, they feel like great experts in the medical field: it is better not to hurt their feelings, so, always show appreciation for this form of attention.

But I do not recommend the pickle juice unless you have a really strong stomach.

Let's disclose the secrets of this chapter

. A lot of verbs to describe the movement, and a few words to describe the parts of the body: what a weird language!

. The names of the body parts are short and easy. To refer to arm and hand you just need a single term, and the same is for leg and foot.

. To describe the traits of the face, there are more specific terms, as well as a lot of adjectives.

. In Russia there are not just blonde people with blue eyes: you better know the other variants too.

. In order to say that you feel pain somewhere, you can use the expression меня болит + subject.

. Russians love giving advices about how to treat sickness: listening to them is a right thing, but taking them literally is your choice!

DAY 26: HOW TO WIN A RUSSIAN HEART

You have known some typical Russian manners, but can you say you deeply understand their nature? It is a difficult challenge for sure, and we cannot understand everything, but some aspects are fundamental in order to establish a good relationship with a Russian. And why not, maybe win his/her heart!

26.1. The Russian character and manners

Russians: cold, unpleasant, indifferent... yes, maybe. But they are also welcoming, playful, thoughtful, sometimes they have some greatness comlex and they are real chatty. Which face do you want to take a look at?
It is hard defining a Russian's character, even thinking about prejudices: if you think about it, every people has a "standard" image in the world; this is really hard with Russians.

We have to admit that, in the last years, the Russian society changed a lot, and so their manners: if kindness and respect are still important values to older people, to a lot of younger people this values have been replaced by richness and "honor". Obviously, this new part of society, the новые русские, new Russians, are a little disliked in the country.

Even before the communist ideology, the sense of community and of the collective action have always been stronger than the emerge of the individual. Modernity has changed a lot of things, wearing out this typical trait of the Russian character too.

Russian men are still used to show gallantry towards women, even if they are colleagues or foreign guests, and they still keep having this really traditional attitude. In the Russian society, women are statistically more than men (according to a survey by the ONU in 2015, there are 86.8 men per 100 women), but their position is still subordinate.
The male foreign tourists first notice the fact that there are more women, giving in to the charm of the Russian women-always flawless, sometimes too much, even when they show off their long dresses in the park or their high heels on the ice!

This attitude of subordination of the woman is reflected in the language too: for example, the verb "to get married" is translated differently for a man and a woman.

жениться с + instrumental= to take sb as your wife (жена)
выходить замуж за + accusative= to go behind a husband (за+муж)

Anyway, to win a Russian heart, you just need some easy moves, as long as they are authentic: these are the first steps to establish an emotional contact with a Russian. In the interpersonal relationships, friendship is a really important value, to which you have to put your heart and soul.
Do not be surprised if Russians love talking about their personal matters: if they do so, it means that they consider you worthy of their trust, and God only knows how much this means to them!

A negative consequence of this situation is that, in Russia, still today, mistrust and secrecy are so common (above all among the older people): after terrible years spent living in the uncertainty, mistrusting everyone, even the neighbors, today it is really hard being open and willing towards foreigners.

Lastly, we have to say also that Russians love giving advices even if they do not know you, even if you won't see them again in your life, even if you do not think you need it, and often, they do it by using a tone that could annoy us: while I was on the subway in Moscow, I was chatting with some friends using a tone of voice that I considered normal. A lady, sat near us, petrified us by saying "тише не можете?", literally "can't you talk quietly?", adding then the fact that we were not in our room.
More forthright than this!

So, as Churchill used to say, "Russia is a rebus wrapped up in a mistery that is kept in an enigma". When I think about the Russian character, I cannot imagine anything different from a matryoshka doll: it may be a predictable image, but definitely a realistic one.

26.2. A true case: national pride

Travelling all over Russia made me think a lot about my country, in terms of pride. Well, to Russians, national pride is a real flag that everyone wave proudly, beyond the different way of thinking.

Russians consider their homeland almost as a person, and attention: in Russian родина is definitely feminine, for this reason they call it Мама Россия, Mother Russia.

Often I was asked the uncomfortable question Чем вы гордитесь в твоей стране?, meaning "what are you proud of in your country?". The verb гордиться, gardìzza, to be proud (reflexive verb), derives from the feminine noun гордость, gòrdast', pride. It is almost a living word, it gives you the idea of being full of pride. And Russians are so proud of a lot of things: first of all, greatness is a real reason to brag.

Largest country in the world, most numerous army of the world, record buildings and huge economic plans. Often, Russians claim to be the inventors of objects that actually are not "made in Russia" (the telephone or the computer!), even if some Russians excel in these fields too- one of the two inventors of Google, Sergej Brin, was from Moscow!

The question of my Russian teacher was followed by an answer that listed everything the Russians are proud of: their traditions, above all the Orthodox Christian ones, their art, their territory and its natural beauties, (земля, the land, that has a really strong value to Russians), but also their scientists and the great minds of their country, writers, philosophers, astronauts, athletes...

To Russians the reasons to brag about their national pride are wasted. You will surely happen to listen to a Russian complaining about his/her own country: in that case, be quiet without agreeing to it, because only Russians can complain about their родина (род- is a really important root contained in a lot of words that refer to the fact of "giving birth", such as родители, parents, and родиться, to be born).

A last curiosity: if World War I is translated literally in Russian as Первая Мировая Война (Piérvaya miravàya vainà), World War II became Великая Отечественная Война (Vielìkaya Atiécesviennaya vainà), "Great patriotic war". Отечество is the other term to indicate the homeland and it is formed on the word отец, atiéz, father.

Let's disclose the secrets of this chapter

. Russians: there is more than a cold heart.

. Kindness and respect are still important values in the modern Russian society, even if sometimes "stumble" in front of modernity.

. The sense of community is also a strong value inside the Russian society.

. Men are less than women, so men, step up! But do not forget gallantry.

. It may seem an intrusive behavior, but Russians love minding someone else's business and giving advices on everything, even if they do not know you.

. In the Russian society, there is still a strong sense of national pride: this is not a light concept when it comes to speak with a Russian.

DAY 27: PLANS FOR THE FUTURE

Until now, you have learned how to use the verbs in the present and in the past tense, paying attention to the aspects too (see chapter 18). Now let's see forward: let's focus on the future tense!

27.1. The compound future tense

The first verb in the future tense that we will study in Russian is the verb "to be": as we have already seen, this verb is "invisible" just in the present tense, but it is visible in the past tense(chap.17) as it is in the future tense too:

я буду	I will be
ты будешь	you will be
он будет	he will be
мы будем	we will be
вы будете	you will be
они будут	they will be

This type of future is really important because it is fundamental to form one of the two future tenses of the Russian language, the future tense compound:
ex. Я буду читать = I will read

subject + v. to be in the future tense + infinite of the verb
This construction is used to express:
- a generic action that will occur in the future:
ex. <u>Завтра</u> он будет читать книгу.
= Tomorrow he will read a book.

- an action that will have a certain duration:
ex. Мы будем заниматься русским языком <u>целое утро</u>.

= We will be studying Russian the whole morning.

- an action that will occur again:
ex. <u>Каждый день</u> вы будете повторять новые слова.
= Everyday you will repeat the new words.

27.2. The simple future tense

Despite the name, the "simple" future is the most complex to form, from a logical point of view. Here, the aspects that you have studied at chapter 18 play a fundamental role. Do you remember what we have said about the perfective? "Perfective: conjugation of the present tense= future tense!!".

ex. Завтра я прочитаю книгу = Tomorrow I <u>will finish to read</u> the book.

So, yes, to form the simple future, you just have to take a verb in its perfective aspect and conjugate it with the suffixes of the present tense: the meaning is a concluded action, distinctive characteristic of the perfective aspect.

Aspectual pair делать-сделать (to do)
compound future tense: я буду делать, ты будешь делать...

simple future tense:
я сделаю
ты сделаешь
он сделает
мы сделаем
вы сделаете
они сделают

Take a look at these two sentences:
Завтра я буду читать книгу.
Завтра я прочитаю книгу.

Both express a future action, that will happen tomorrow (Завтра, sàvtra). The difference is in the type of action: the future with буду just indicates the the action that will occur, on the contrary, the future with the perfective, indicates the will to complete an action.

The Russian language is so meticulous on the use of aspects and the rules may seem a lot, but we can schematize every-thing in a table:

Tab. 12: RECAP OF THE USE OF CASES

	HCB/imperfective	CB/perfective
PRESENT	incomplete action	completed action
	я читаю= I read	-
PAST	я читал= I read	я прочитал= I have read (finished reading)
FUTURE	я буду читать= I will read	я прочитаю= I will finish reading

Lastly, as it happened with the verb to be in the past tense, even the verb to be in the future tense is followed by the instrumental case: take a look at it

Он был писателем = he was a writer
Он будет писателем = he will be a writer

If you add an adjective (главный = important) to the noun писатель, it must be in the instrumental case:
Он был главным писателем
Он будет главным писателем

Besides these two cases (v. to be in the past and in the future tense), there is another verb that follows the same rules and it is followed by the instrumental: this is the verb "to become", становиться-стать. In the exercises you just have the perfective form стать conjugated in the past or in the simple future tense.

EXERCISE 25

Complete the sentences with the <u>instrumental</u> of the noun or the adjective in brackets

1. Когда Катя была _____ (маленькая), она хотела стать _____ (известная журналистка).

2. Он будет _____ (счастливый), только когда он защитит диплом.

3. Мы стали _____ (грустные), потому что каникули закончили.

4. Настя и Ольга будут _____ (студентки), когда они будут в университете.

5. Вы были _____ (хорошие школьники), когда вы были в школе.

EXERCISE 26

Make the future of both types for the pairs of the given verbs: remember the consonant alternations (chapter 10)
ex. помогать – помочь: я буду помогать / я помогу

1. готовить - приготовить
2. курить - покурить
3. есть – съесть (irregular! See chapter 10.3)
4. пить - выпить
5. спать - проспать
6. писать – написать

EXERCISE 27

Past-Present-Future: change the sentences... but be careful to the aspect!

past:
Он <u>работал</u> всю ночь
present:
Он <u>работает</u> всю ночь
future:
Он <u>будет работать</u> всю ночь

Past: ...
Present: Вы быстро <u>ездите</u> на велосипеде. (imperfective)
Future: ...

Past: Мы <u>купили</u> цветы. (perfective)
Present: ...
Future: ...

Past: ...
Present: ...
Future: Мы <u>поедем</u> в России. (perfective)

Past: Она всегда <u>поела</u> русские песни. (imperfective)
Present: ...
Future: ...

If you do not remember some verbs, take a look at chapter 18.

Let's disclose the secrets of this chapter

. In Russian there are two types of future, the compound and the simple one.

. The compound future is formed with the future of the verb to be (буду, будешь, …) + imperfective infinitive.

. The compound future indicates an action that will take place in the future but in a generic way.

. The simple future is formed by conjugating the perfective infinitive: прочитать →прочитаю, прчитаешь,…

. The simple future indicates the actions when they are concluded.

. As the past tense, the future too is followed by the instrumental case: you can use this construction to say what you have been (я был ребёнком, I was a child) and what you will be (я буду счастливым человеком, I will be a happy person).

ANSWERS.

Exercise 25
1. маленькой - известной журналисткой.
When Katya was a younger, she wanted to become a famous journalist.
2. счастливым.
He will be happy just when he will be graduated
3. грустными.
We have become sad because the holidays are over.
4. студентками.
Nastya and Olga will become students when they will go to the university.
5. хорошими школьниками.
You were good schoolchildren when you were at school.

Exercise 26
1. готовить — приготовить: я буду готовить / я приготовлю, ты приготовишь, ...
2. курить — покурить: я буду курить / я покурю
3. есть — съесть: я буду есть / я съем, ты съешь, он съест...
4. пить — выпить: я буду пить / я выпью, ты выпьёшь
5. спать — поспать: я буду спать / я посплю, ты поспишь,...
6. писать — написать: я буду писать / я напишу, ты напишешь, ...

Exercise 27
Past: ЕЗДИЛИ
Present: Вы быстро <u>ездите</u> на велосипеде.
Future: БУДЕТЕ ЕЗДИТЬ

Past: Мы <u>купили</u> цветы.
Present: ПОКУПАЕМ*
Future: КУПИМ

Past: ПОЕХАЛИ
Present: ЕДЕМ *
Future: Мы <u>поедем</u> в России.

Past: Она всегда <u>поела</u> русские песни.
Present: ПОЁТ
Future: БУДЕТ ПЕТЬ

* Remember: the present tense can be formed just with the verbs in the imperfective case. The conjugation of the perfective "present" actually corresponds to the future tense

DAY 28: PARTY TIME!

You are getting closer and closer to the end of your thirty days Russian language course and now it is time to celebrate like a proper Russian!

Attention: it is not exactly as Robbie Williams describes it in "Party Like A Russian" ... not always at least!

28.1. Religion and nation

In Russia there are plenty of situations to celebrate something, and people love spending these moments together: whatever the situation, the key to a good party is fun.

We can divide the main Russian celebrations in two groups, the religious ones and those linked to the history of the nation.

The religious celebrations are linked to the Orthodox calendar that is 13 days late in comparison with our calendar: for this reason, the Russian Christmas falls on the 6th of January; at the same time, though, Russians celebrate New Year's Eve as we do, between the 31st of December and the 1st of January!

To avoid any kind of confusion, here a list of the main religious celebrations:

1st of January: Новый Год, New Year's Eve

6th of January: Рождество, Christmas

23rd of February: День защитника Отечества, Defender of the Fatherland Day, or "men day"

8th of March: Женский день, Women's Day

April/ May: Православная Пасха, Orthodox Easter

1st of May: День труда, Labor Day

9th of May: День победы, Victory Day, to remember the victory on the Nazis during the World War II

12th of June: День России, Indipendence Day

7th of November: День согласия и примирения, Reconciliation and national harmony Day, in the past this was the anniversay of the October Revolution

12th of December: День Коституции, Constitution Day, a celebration established recently.

As you can see, a lot of celebrations linked to the nation remained the same during the different historical periods, but their names or the object of the same celebration changed. So, today, the famous "Defender of the Fatherland Day"is a celebration belonging to the army, but it is also a real "man day", thought to be almost as an equivalent of the 8th of March.

There are also a lot of rituals linked to the religious celebrations that take inspiration from the Orthodox Christian church: apart from the difference in the calendar that I mentioned earlier, there are also a lot of periods that precede the celebrations: the fastings of the Advent and of the Lent, or Масленица, a sort of Orthodox Mardi Gras, so beloved to adults and children,and often represented in the pagan popular tradition as a celebration to welcome Spring (it is usually celebrated during the month of March).

Every city has its peculiar celebrations, and some of them are followed up by a great number of people: more than once, I took part in the celebrations of the "Navy Day" that falls on the last Sunday of July: everyone take part in this celebration, included the students of the Navy military schools. The celebrations involve every citizen between rivers of beer and vodka that sometimes give rise to more or less friendly scuffles: it is better knowing when it is time to leave in this case!

In order to give somebody one's best wishes, this grammatical construction can be really useful:

С + Instrumental

ex. С Рождеством!

Attention: день in the instrumental case becomes ДНЁМ because the vowel disappears.

С днём победы!
Happy "Victory Day"!

28.2. The most beloved celebration

The birthday celebration is part of the Russian tradition and it definitely is the most beloved celebration: it is a special moment for families that gather around the birthday boy/girl creating a joyful and thrilling atmosphere. There is always plenty of food, the cake with the candles and also the gifts have an important role, even if they always have to go with a handwritten greeting card (never buy a pre-printed greeting card to a Russian! It would be an awful act of carelessness towards someone).

Well, the celebrations are similar to ours, with the song on the same notes of "happy birthday to you":

С днём рождения тебя!
С днём рождения тебя!
С днём рождения, с днём рождения
С днём рождения тебя!

The pronunciation is reduced and some letters are not pronunciated: "S niòm rajdiénia tibià".

If you want to say how old you are, you have to use an expression in the dative case:
МНЕ + 1, 21, 31, 41, ... + год
МНЕ + 2, 3, 4, 22, 23, 24, ... + года
МНЕ + (from 5 on, aside from the special cases) + лет

Ex. Мне 21 год. Тебе 44 года. А Ивану 15 лет

If you do not understand these partitions, step back and take a look at the chapter about numbers(chapter 22). To review the personal pronouns in the dative case, take a look at chapter 7, table 5.

Let's disclose the secrets of this chapter

. Russians love celebrating and there are a lot of occasions to do that.

. The religious traditional celebrations follow the Orthodox calendar, 13 days behind in comparison with ours.

. There are a lot of national celebrations, and the majority of them were established during the Soviet era and then "reaccustomed".

. In order to give somebody your best wishes, you have to use the construction C + Instrumental.

. The birthday, день рождения, is a celebration similar to ours.

. If you want to express the age in Russian, you have to use the dative followed by the number with год / года / лет (=years old) depending on the number (the numbers ending with 1, год; the numbers ending with 2,3 and 4 – except for 12,13 and 14- are followed by года; the numbers ending with 5 or other numbers- 12, 13 and 14 included, that we have left out earlier- are followed by лет.

DAY 29: THE ATOMS OF THE SENTENCE

In the Russian language there are a lot of short words that escape the big net of grammar: they are above all brief words that never change with the annoying masculine, feminine etc. nouns.

In this large group of short words we can distinguish three families: conjunctions, prepositions and particles.

Meaningful sentences can also be composed of just a few particles, such as ну and же, that taken singularly do not have a defined meaning. We will focus on them on point 29.3 of this lesson. The sentence in this cartoon basically mean: "And here I am".

29.1. Conjunctions

It is not hard to memorize these short words that are useful for the sentence: let's see a first group of conjunctions, similar in the meaning, but that transmit a slightly different hint

И = and   (У меня есть кошка и собака = I have a cat and a dog)

А = while, on the contrary (У меня есть кошка, а у тебя есть собака = I have a cat, while you have a dog)

НО = but (У меня есть кошка, но я хочу собаку = I have a cat, but I want a dog)

Another group concerns the different ways to say "too, also":

ТАКЖЕ = also (two different actions)- Я читаю газету, а также разговариваю с тобой.

ТОЖЕ = too (equally: two identical actions or situations)- Я читаю газеты и тоже книги.

ЕЩЁ = too / yet – Я купила ещё газету.

Lastly, an important word is "why/because": in the questions you have to use "Почему?", in the answers you have to say Потому что...

- Почему ты взял зонтик?
- Потому что шёл дождь.
(Why did you take the umbrella? Because it rained).

29.2. Prepositions

During our lessons, we have already seen a lot of prepositions with their own rections. Here I want to give you a conclusive scheme of all the main prepositions depending on the case that is followed:

Tab. 13: PREPOSITIONS AND CASES

Genitive

у= by
около/близко от= nearby, close by
далеко от= far away from
из/с= from (to move away from a place: из for a closed space and с for an open space)
от= from sb (письмо от друга)
до= until
без= without
для= for

Dative

к= towards
по= on a surface

Accusative

в/на= movement to a place

Instrumental

с= by, with
над= over
под= under
перед= in front of
за= behind
между= between

Prepositional

в/на= they specify the place and also the time in which an action takes place
о= about sth or sb

Remember that when they are pronounced, the prepositions composed of one or two letters are never stressed: so, expressions like до свидания are pronounced "dasvidània" as they were a single word.

As a consequence, in the written text the preposition can be recognized more easily in comparison with the speech.

EXERCISE 28

Try to read these expressions keeping in mind that the brief prepositions are never stressed. Answers at the end of the chapter.

письмо от друга;
говорить о Москве;
мост над рекой;
мы с друзьями;
дядя из Рима.
плыть по озеру;
картина у бабушки;
до встреча

29.3. Particles

Maybe, the the particles are the most difficult thing to learn for a foreigner studying Russian: short words apparently harmless, but real brain-teasers that a lot of academics did not manage to define once and for all.

It is like that the handbook about the use of particles - if there is one- is downloaded in the DNA of each Russian at the moment of the birth, and often, they cannot explain why they are using them.

One of my favourites is ЖЕ: we could call it "intensifier", we could say that it points out a concept already expressed inside the sentence, but it could also be a lot of other things. Let's see it in action:

- Почему ты взял мне эту книгу?
- Ты <u>же</u> сам мне сказал.

- Why did you bring me that book?
- Well, you told me to do it.

You can use же when you want to eamphasize a sentence, even more than the intonation.

Another common particle is ведь: its meaning can be translated as "for sure", "surely", emphasizing the sentence.
- Ты идёшь на вечеринку?
- Но <u>ведь</u> я не могу отказаться

. Are you going to the party?
- Well, I surely cannot refuse it.

Lastly, there is вот, common in the speech, that can be translated as "here", often combined with ну, a mix between "let's go" and "come on", but it can have dfferent meanings depending on the tone:

Вот новость! = here a news!

Ну вот ещё! = but what are you talking about? - well, really! (with a derogatory tone)

We have to devote another special mention to ну that you have seen in action in this last sentence: you could write a lot of books about ну! "Nu" is especially used in the speech, it is often combined with "da" (yes) to give a hint of obviousness to the answer that you are giving to an interlocutor:

- Did you buy vodka for the party?
- Nu da!

It is usually placed at the beginning of sentences or it is inserted as a parenthetical element between two commas. I have learned to pronounce it as a "filling word" when I do not know how to switch concept, or to review the conclusive parts of an argument. Versatile!

Let's disclose the secrets of this chapter

. In the Russian language there are words that stay intact and never change: these are the conjunctions, the prepositions and the particles.

. The conjunctions are numerous and they are studied in groups of similar meanings, such as "and", "but" and "also".

. Each preposition is followed by different cases, or even by more than one case with different meanings.

. The prepositions of one or two letters are never stressed, and in the pronunciation, they "attach" to the word that they introduce: ex. до свидания = dasvidània

. The particles are so difficult to interpret for a non-mother tongue.

. Among the common particles, the most used ones in the speech, there are же and ведь with an intensifying idea, вот to introduce something, and ну, a sort of a stock phrase, often repeated by Russians to start sentences too.

ANSWERS.

Exercise 28

pismò at-drùga;
gavarìt' a-Maskvié;
most nad-rikòi;
my s-drusiàmi;
diàdia is-Rìma;
plyt' pa-òsieru;
kartìna u-bàbushki;
da-vstriécha.

DAY 30: YOUR FIRST TRIP TO RUSSIA

We are at the end of this brief journey inside the Russian language. But we are also at the beginning of a new adventure, that is to say how to put into practice what you have learned on the real field: Russia.

30.1. Golden advices

Before packing your suitcases, I want to give you a few more useful advices if you ever happen to visit this country: it is about things that I have already said during this course, and that now I gather in a single list:

1. BE ALWAYS PATIENT AND HAVE ADAPTABIL-ITY: these are two important qualities that you must have if you want to visit Russia. Just with this spirit you will be able to appreciate the beauties of this country;

2. DO NOT BE SCARED TO TRY: try to speak, try to look at things with a different point of view, but also try new flavours and new experiences. This advice is more a motto, but keep it in mind: Russia changes you, whether you like it or not.

3. SHOW RESPECT: an arrogant behavior never helped nobody abroad, even less in Russia. Before giving your best, make sure to be in the right territory to do it. In the interpersonal relationships, respecting the other is a good habit and an essential one to start off on the right foot. To overcome formality, though, it is better letting the Russians do the first step. Sometimes, expansiveness can upset them.

4. WHEN IN RUSSIA, DO LIKE THE RUSSIANS DO: this does not mean "forget your origins", nor "try to stick to them like a stamp": you have to give Russia a chance, and do not wait for her to do the first step.

5. SPEAK RUSSIAN, A LOT AND ALWAYS: nobody will have problems with your non-perfect accent, and if you do not remember exactly that word that you are looking for, don't worry. Once, at a restaurant, I wanted a dish with

mushrooms and I said to the waiter that I was "going mush-rooming" because I got the wrong preposition: we all laughed and I got my dish with mushrooms. Beautiful things too can be born from a mistake, (such as the mushroom pi-rojki).

30.2. Letter from a friend

As a last exercise, you have to translate a letter from an American student in Russia, Edward, to his friends John and Mary. In the text you may find some words that you do not know. The complete translation of the letter is at the end of the chapter, after the secrets.

Письмо от друга = a letter from a friend

"Здравствуй, Джон! Как дела, друг? Я часто думаю о тебе и о Мери и очень скучаю по (= mi manca) нашему городу.

Я уже два месяца живу в Москве. Москва — город огромный. Культурный центр! Столица! (=capital city). Здесь много баров, кафе, ресторанов, ночных клубов, кинотеатров, театров, музеев и магазинов. И очень много красивых женщин.

Везде (= everywhere) — в кафе и в барах, в музеях и в ресторанах, на улицах и площадях, на проспектах и в переулках (along boulevards and in the streests) — можно встретить иностранцев. Я познакомился здесь с японцами, испанцами, корейцами, итальянцами, турками, китайцами, англичанами, арабами, французами и, конечно, с американцами. Здесь очень много наших соотечественников (= compatriots). Я своим новым знакомым рассказываю о своей (= my own, свой, used in the following sentences too) стране, о своём родном городе, о своих друзьях, а они мне рассказывают о своих городах и странах. Очень интересно!

Русские в Москве тоже есть. Например, наши преподаватели (= teachers). Я писал тебе, что учусь на курсах русского языка? У нас в группе два преподавателя.

Они очень любопытные (= curious), задают много вопросов (= the ask a lot of questions): "У вас большая семья? А сколько у вас братьев? А сестёр? А друзей? А где вы были вчера? А с кем вы там были? Что вы там делали? Куда вы пойдёте завтра? С кем вы туда пойдёте?" Ещё я думаю, что наши преподаватели очень любят путешествовать (= travelling). Почему я так думаю? Потому что они собирают информацию (= they gather info) о разных городах и странах. Они спрашивают: "Из какого города вы приехали? Где находится ваш город? Какая в вашем городе погода зимой, весной, осенью и летом? Сколько в вашем городе улиц, площадей, музеев, театров, магазинов, ресторанов, баров, кафе, больниц, парков, школ, университетов, гостиниц, стадионов, домов, машин?"

Очень любознательные (= curious, in a positive way: composed of любить+ знать, to love + to know) люди.

Напиши мне (= write me back), пожалуйста, о наших друзьях и подругах, о твоих планах на будущее.

Твой друг

Эдвард

P.S. Не говори Мери, что в Москве много красивых женщин!"

Let's disclose the secrets of this chapter

. There is no better way to implement the study of a language than putting it into practice on the field.

. You have to remember to be patient and to have always adaptability.

. Try, try, try, try: just by doing so you can improve.

. The respect of the other and of his/her times are the key to a good relationship, in Russia more than ever.

. Get mixed up with Russians, try to go unnoticed among them and study their behaviors.

. A foreign language is made to be spoken, listened, understood or barely mumbled too: you have to try anyway!

ANSWER

Hi John! How are you my friend? I often think about you and Mary and I really miss our city. I have been living in Moscow for two months already. Moscow is a huge city. A cultural center! A capital city! Here there are a lot of cafès, restaurants, discotheques, cinemas, theaters, museums and shops. And beautiful women too.

Everywhere – inside cafès, museums, restaurants, in the streets, on squares, along boulevards and alleys – you can meet foreigners. I have met people from Japan, Spain, Korea, Italy, Turkey, China, England, Arabia, France and obviously from America. Here there are a lot of our compatriots. I tell my new acquaintances about my country, my city, my friends, and they tell me about their cities and countries. It is really interesting!

Clearly, in Moscow there are also Russians. For example, our teachers. Did I mention the fact that I study in a class of Russian language? In our group there are two teachers. They are so curious and they ask a lot of questions. "Do you have a large family? And how many brothers do you have? How many sisters? And what about friends? And where have you been yesterday? With who have you been? What have you done? Where are you going tomorrow? With who?".

I think that our teachers love travelling. Why do I think so? Because they gather information about the different cities and countries we come from. They ask us: "What city do you come from? Where is it? How is the weather there during winter, spring, fall and summer? How many streets, squares, museums, theaters, shops, restaurants, cafès, hospitals, parks, schools, universities, hotels, stadiums, houses, cars are there?

They are really curious people.

Write me back about our friends and about your plans for the future.

Your friend,
Edward
ps: Don't tell Mary that in Moscow there are a lot of beautiful women!

CONCLUSIONS

You got to the end of this textbook and first of all you deserve my congratulations: completing a task with a foreign language is not always easy, and you need a good mix of perseverance and patience.

It does not end here, though: you can decide to expand your study in different ways, from grammar textbooks to the tutorial videos on YouTube, but my most sincere advice is establishing a relationship with a mother tongue person, that could help you in this trip in the Russian language.
Well, it is obvious, as I have already pointed out during our lessons, travelling to Russia is another fundamental step to keep studying the language.

Together we have already made a lot of fundamental steps necessary to a good comprehension of the Russian language. In your work with this language, tools like a dictionary, pocket-sized too, and a grammar textbook cannot be missed: on the market there are a lot of options and the choice can be hard. I recommend avoiding "hard" grammar textbooks and with too much regard to the contents, favoring more fluid ones and full of practical exercises, better with audio/video support.
For everything else, you cannot know a language withouth knowing its culture, so, fling yourself as soon as possible in this discovery: come back to the chapter 22 for the advices on books, and do not miss the weekly episode of "Masha and the Bear"- obviusly in the original version!

If, on the contrary, you are an intrepid reader and this textbook raised in you the desire to speak Russian from morning to night, you can always consider a course – and why not, in Russia even!

Do not miss the chance of discovering closer this wonderful culture: I assure you, there will be a lot of suprises.

Have a nice trip in the Russian language!

TABLES SUMMARY

Tab. 1: THE CYRILLIC ALPHABET

Cyrillic Letter	Cursive Writing	Pronunciation	Scientific Transliteration	Examples	Translation
А а	А а	a	a	аэропорт	airport
Б б	Б б	b	b	брат	brother
В в	В в	v	v	вагон	wagon
Г г	Г г	g (strong)	g	гараж	garage
Д д	Д д	d	d	да	yes
Е е	Е е	ye as in "yes"	e	есть	to eat
Ё ё	Ё ё	yo as in "yolk"	ё	ёж	hedgehog
Ж ж	Ж ж	"j" in French word "jour"	zh	жена	wife
З з	З з	z as in "zoo"	z	зоопарк	zoo
И и	И и	i	i	игра	game
Й й	Й й	(short i) as in boy	i	йогурт	yogurt
К к	К к	k	k	кошка	cat
Л л	Л л	l	l	луна	moon
М м	М м	m	m	мама	mom
Н н	Н н	n	n	нет	no
О о	О о	o (closed)	o	опера	opera
П п	П п	p	p	папа	dad
Р р	Р р	r	r	Россия	Russia
С с	С с	s	s	студент	student
Т т	Т т	t	t	туфли	shoes
У у	У у	u	u	университет	university
Ф ф	Ф ф	f	f	фото	photo
Х х	Х х	aspirated cha s in German "Achtung"	kh	характер	character
Ц ц	Ц ц	ts as in "tsunami"	ts	цирк	circus
Ч ч	Ч ч	ch as in "cheese"	ch	чай	tea
Ш ш	Ш ш	sh as in "shock"	sh	шуба	fur
Щ щ	Щ щ	shsh as in "fresh sheen" but softer	shch	щётка	hairbrush
ъ	ъ	hard sign	-	-	-
ы	ы	i (strong)	y	дыр	hole
ь	ь	soft sign	-	-	-
Э э	Э э	e with the mouth open wider	è	экзамен	exam
Ю ю	Ю ю	yu as in "Yukon"	yu	юбка	skirt
Я я	Я я	ya as in "Yalta"	ya	яблоко	apple

Tab. 2: CONSONANTS AND VOWELS SUMMARY

hard	б в г д з л м н п р с т ф х (followed by a hard vowel or, rarely, hard sign) + а э ы о у + ъ	ж ш ц	
soft	б в г д з л м н п р с т ф х (followed by a soft vowel and/or soft sign) +я е и ё ю + ь		ч щ

Tab. 3: DECLENSION OF NOUNS IN THE SINGULAR

gender	case	hard			soft		
M	Nom	стол	stol	the table	конь	kogn	horse
	Gen	стола	stalà	of the table	коня	kagnià	of the horse
	Dat	столу	stalù	to the table	коню	kagniù	to the horse
	Acc	стол	stol	the table (dir.obj)	коня*	kagnià	the horse (dir.obj)
	Instrum	столом	stalòm	with the table	конём	kagniàm	with the horse
	Prep	столе	staliè	(on) the table	коне	kagniè	(on) the horse
N	Nom	село	sielò	the village	море	mòrie	the sea
	Gen	села	sielà	of the village	моря	mòria	of the sea
	Dat	селу	sielù	to the village	морю	mòriu	to the sea
	Acc	село	sielò	the village (dir.obj)	море	mòrie	the sea (dir.obj)
	Instrum	селом	sielòm	with the village	морём	mariòm	with the sea
	Prep	селе	sieliè	(in) the village	море	mòrie	(in) the sea
F	Nom	мама	màma	mom	тётя	tiòtia	the aunt
	Gen	мамы	màmy	mom's (Eng. Possessive)	тёти	tiòti	aunt's (Eng. Possessive)
	Dat	маме	màmie	to mom	тёте	tiòtie	to the aunt
	Acc	маму	màmu	mom (dir.obj)	тётю	tiòtiu	the aunt (dir.obj)
	Instrum	мамой	màmai	with mom	тётей	tiòtiei	with the aunt
	Prep	маме	màmie	(about) mom	тёте	tiòtie	(about) the aunt

Tab. 4: DECLENSION OF NOUNS IN THE PLURAL

gender	case	hard			soft		
M	Nom	Столы	stalí	the tables	Кони	kagní	the horses
	Gen	Столов	stalòv	of the tables	Коней	kagnièi	of the horses
	Dat	Столам	stalàm	to the tables	Коням	kagniàm	to the horses
	Acc	Столы	stalí	the tables (dir.obj.)	Коней*	kagniéi	the horses (dir.obj)
	Instrum	Столами	stalàmi	with the tables	Конями	kagniàmi	with the horses
	Prep	Столах	stalàkh	(on) the tables	Конях	kagniakh	(on) the horses
N	Nom	Сёла	siòla	the villages	Моря	marià	the seas
	Gen	Сёл	siòl	of the villages	Морей	marièi	of the seas
	Dat	Сёлам	siòlam	to the villages	Морям	mariàm	to the seas
	Acc	Сёла	siòla	the villages (dir.obj)	Моря	marià	the seas (dir.obj)
	Instrum	Сёлами	siòlami	with the villages	Морями	mariàmi	with the seas
	Prep	Сёлах	siòlakh	(in) the villages	Морях	mariàkh	(in) the seas
F	Nom	Мамы	màmy.	the moms	Тёти	tiòti	the aunts
	Gen	Мам	mam.	moms'	Тёть*	tiòt'	aunts'
	Dat	Мамам	màmama	to the moms	Тётям	tiòtiam	to the aunts
	Acc	мам*	mam.	the moms (dir.obj)	тёть*	tiòt'	the aunts (dir.obj)
	Instrum	мамами	màmami.	with the moms	тётями	tiòtiami	with the aunts
	Prep	мамах	màmakh.	(about) the moms	тётях	tiòtiakh	(about) the aunts

339

Tab. 5: PERSONAL PRONOUNS IN NOMINATIVE, GENITIVE AND DATIVE

	nominative		genitive		dative	
I- me- to me	Я	Yà	Меня	minyà	Мне	mniè
You- you- to you	Ты	ty	Тебя	tibyà	Тебе	tibiè
He- him- to him	Он	on	(н)его	n-ievò	Ему	iemù
She- her- to her	Она	anà	(н)её	n-ieiò	Eй	ièi
It- it- to it	Оно	anò	(н)его	n-ievò	Ему	iemù
We- us - to us	Мы	my	Нас	nas	Нам	nam
You- you- to you	Вы	vy	Вас	vas	Вам	vam
They- them - to them	Они	ani	(н)их	n-ich	Им	im

Tab. 6: THE 7 INTONATIONS AND THEIR USE

ИК-1 *declarative sentences:*

Это моя мама

ИК-2 *interrogative sentences introduced by adverbs:*

Где ваша собака?

ИК-3 *generic interrogative sentences:*

(the tone goes upt and then becomes flat again)

У тебя есть ручка?= *do you have a pen?*

ИК-4 *interrogative sentences that point out a comparison:*
(the tone is higher than the 3)

А ты?= *and you?*

ИК-5 *interjections introduced by "как/какой" (=what):*

Какая погода!= *what a wonderful weather!*

ИК-6 *enthusiasm interjection:*

(the tone goes up and it stays high)

Как весело!= *that's wonderful!*

ИК-7 *ironic-derogatory interjection:*

Какие они друзья!= *what friends!*

Tab. 7: POSSESSIVE ADJECTIVES IN THE NOMINATIVE

	M		F		N		PL	
my	Мой	mòi	Моя	mayà	Моё	mayò	Мои	maì
your	Твой	tvòi	Твоя	tvayà	Твоё	tvayò	Твои	tvai
his	Его	ievò	Его		ero		ero	
her	Её	ieyò	Её		её		её	
its	Его	ievò	Его		ero		ero	
our	Наш	nash	Наша	nasha	Наше	nashe	Наши	nàshi
your	Ваш	vash	Ваша	vasha	Ваше	vashe	Ваши	vàshi
their	Их	ich	Их		Их		Их	

Tab. 8: THE DECLENSION OF ADJECTIVES

Case	M soft/hard	F soft/hard	N soft/hard	PL soft/hard
Nominative	-ий or -ой/-ий	-ая/-яя	-ое/-ее	-ые/-ие
Genitive	-ого/-его	-ой/-ей	-ого/-его	-ых/их
Dative	-ому/-ему	-ой/-ей	-ому/-ему	-ым/им
Accusative	=Nom or Gen*	-ую/-юю	=Nom	=Nom or Gen*
Instrumental	-ым/-им	-ой/-ей	-ым/-им	-ыми/-ими
Prepositional	-ом/-ем	-ой/ей	-ом/-ем	-ых/-их

*= Nom. is the noun is inanimated; =Gen. if the noun is animated.

Tab. 9: CONSONANT ALTERNATION IN VERBS

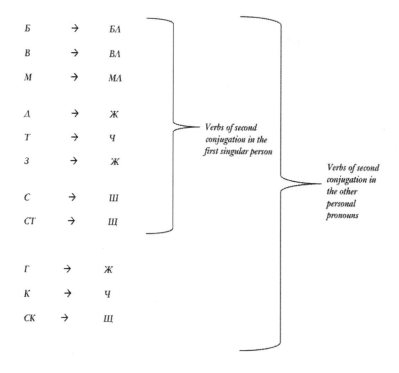

Б	→	БЛ
В	→	ВЛ
М	→	МЛ
Д	→	Ж
Т	→	Ч
З	→	Ж
С	→	Ш
СТ	→	Щ
Г	→	Ж
К	→	Ч
СК	→	Щ

Verbs of second conjugation in the first singular person

Verbs of second conjugation in the other personal pronouns

Tab. 10: THE MAIN VERBS OF MOTION AND THEIR MEANING (pay attention: they are all imperfectives)

monodirectional:

pluridirectional:

идти	to walk/to go on foot	ходить
ехать	to move using a vehicle	ездить
бежать	to run	бегать
лететь.	to fly	летать
плыть	to swim	плавать
нести	to carry an object in hands	носить
вести	to carry sth/sb , to drive	водить
везти	to carry sth, to transport	возить

Tab. 11: PREPOSITIONS OF PLACE AND GOVERNMENTS

около/ недалеко от/ близко= nearby, close by

далеко= far away

от...до= from...to/until...   **+GENITIVE**

y=by

из/с= from

в/на= in, inside   **+ PREPOSITIONAL**

в/на= towards, to (movement towards a place)

за= beyond   **+ACCUSATIVE**

через= through

к= towards (moving closer to sth/sb)

по= through, by   **+DATIVE**

Tab. 12: RECAP OF THE USE OF CASES

	HCB/imperfective	CB/perfective
PRESENT	incomplete action	completed action
	я читаю= I read	-
PAST	я читал= I read	я прочитал= I have read (finished reading)
FUTURE	я буду читать= I will read	я прочитаю= I will finish reading

Tab. 13: PREPOSITIONS AND CASES

Genitive

у= by
около/близко от= nearby, close by
далеко от= far away from
из/с= from (to move away from a place: из for a closed space and с for an open space)
от= from sb (письмо от друга)
до= until
без= without
для= for

Dative

к= towards
по= on a surface

Accusative

в/на= movement to a place

Instrumental

с= by, with
над= over
под= under
перед= in front of
за= behind
между= between

Prepositional

в/на= they specify the place and also the time
in which an action takes place
о= about sth or sb

Made in United States
Orlando, FL
02 June 2023

33739914R00209